THIS BOOK BELONGS TO

EMAIL: ___________________________

ADDRESS: _________________________

CONTACT: _________________________

PHONE: ___________________________

START DATE	END DATE

MO TU WE TH FR SA SU
☐   ☐   ☐   ☐   ☐   ☐   ☐

DATE: _____ / _____ / _____

PROJECT:

FOREMAN:

WEATHER

F°_____ C°_____ _____ AM _____ PM

HOURS DUE TO BAD WEATHER

ISSUED AND DELAYS

NOTE: ____

COMPLETION DATE	DAYS AHEAD OF SCHEDULE	DAYS BEHIND SCHEDULE

SAFETY AND INCIDENTS

SAFETY ISSUES THAT NEED TO BE ADDRESSED	ACCIDENTS / INCIDENTS / STEPS NEEDED TO RESOLVE

SUMMARY OF THE WORK DONE TODAY

IMPORTANT NOTES

NAME	SIGNATURE

<table>
<tr><td colspan="7" align="center">TODAY LABOR</td></tr>
<tr><td>INITIALS</td><td>TRADE</td><td>START</td><td>FINISH</td><td>PAID HOURS</td><td>OVERTIME</td><td>COMPANY</td></tr>
<tr><td>☐ EMPLOYEE
☐ CONTRUCTOR</td><td></td><td>AM</td><td>PM</td><td></td><td></td><td></td></tr>
<tr><td>☐ EMPLOYEE
☐ CONTRUCTOR</td><td></td><td>AM</td><td>PM</td><td></td><td></td><td></td></tr>
<tr><td>☐ EMPLOYEE
☐ CONTRUCTOR</td><td></td><td>AM</td><td>PM</td><td></td><td></td><td></td></tr>
<tr><td>☐ EMPLOYEE
☐ CONTRUCTOR</td><td></td><td>AM</td><td>PM</td><td></td><td></td><td></td></tr>
<tr><td>☐ EMPLOYEE
☐ CONTRUCTOR</td><td></td><td>AM</td><td>PM</td><td></td><td></td><td></td></tr>
<tr><td>☐ EMPLOYEE
☐ CONTRUCTOR</td><td></td><td>AM</td><td>PM</td><td></td><td></td><td></td></tr>
<tr><td>☐ EMPLOYEE
☐ CONTRUCTOR</td><td></td><td>AM</td><td>PM</td><td></td><td></td><td></td></tr>
<tr><td>☐ EMPLOYEE
☐ CONTRUCTOR</td><td></td><td>AM</td><td>PM</td><td></td><td></td><td></td></tr>
</table>

EQUIPMENT ON SITE	NO. OF UNITE	WORKING YES / NO

HIRED EQUIPMENT	NO. OF UNITE	EQUIPMENT RENTED	FROM	RATE

NAME: _______________________   SIGNATURE: _______________________

MO   TU   WE   TH   FR   SA   SU
☐   ☐   ☐   ☐   ☐   ☐   ☐

DATE: /   /

PROJECT:

FOREMAN:

WEATHER   F°_____   C°_____   _____ AM   _____ PM

HOURS DUE TO BAD WEATHER

ISSUED AND DELAYS

NOTE: ____

COMPLETION DATE	DAYS AHEAD OF SCHEDULE	DAYS BEHIND SCHEDULE

SAFETY AND INCIDENTS

SAFETY ISSUES THAT NEED TO BE ADDRESSED	ACCIDENTS / INCIDENTS / STEPS NEEDED TO RESOLVE

SUMMARY OF THE WORK DONE TODAY

IMPORTANT NOTES

NAME	SIGNATURE

TODAY LABOR

INITIALS	TRADE	START	FINISH	PAID HOURS	OVERTIME	COMPANY
☐ EMPLOYEE ☐ CONTRUCTOR		AM	PM			
☐ EMPLOYEE ☐ CONTRUCTOR		AM	PM			
☐ EMPLOYEE ☐ CONTRUCTOR		AM	PM			
☐ EMPLOYEE ☐ CONTRUCTOR		AM	PM			
☐ EMPLOYEE ☐ CONTRUCTOR		AM	PM			
☐ EMPLOYEE ☐ CONTRUCTOR		AM	PM			
☐ EMPLOYEE ☐ CONTRUCTOR		AM	PM			
☐ EMPLOYEE ☐ CONTRUCTOR		AM	PM			

EQUIPMENT ON SITE	NO. OF UNITE	WORKING YES / NO

HIRED EQUIPMENT	NO. OF UNITE	EQUIPMENT RENTED	FROM	RATE

NAME: _______________________   SIGNATURE: _______________________

MO TU WE TH FR SA SU
☐   ☐   ☐   ☐   ☐   ☐   ☐

DATE: /   /

PROJECT:

FOREMAN:

WEATHER

F° _____ C° _____   _____ AM   _____ PM

HOURS DUE TO BAD WEATHER

ISSUED AND DELAYS

NOTE: _________________________________

COMPLETION DATE	DAYS AHEAD OF SCHEDULE	DAYS BEHIND SCHEDULE

SAFETY AND INCIDENTS

SAFETY ISSUES THAT NEED TO BE ADDRESSED	ACCIDENTS / INCIDENTS / STEPS NEEDED TO RESOLVE

SUMMARY OF THE WORK DONE TODAY

IMPORTANT NOTES

NAME	SIGNATURE

<table>
<tr><th colspan="8" align="center">TODAY LABOR</th></tr>
<tr><th>INITIALS</th><th>TRADE</th><th>START</th><th>FINISH</th><th>PAID HOURS</th><th>OVERTIME</th><th>COMPANY</th></tr>
<tr><td>☐ EMPLOYEE
☐ CONTRUCTOR</td><td></td><td>AM</td><td>PM</td><td></td><td></td><td></td></tr>
<tr><td>☐ EMPLOYEE
☐ CONTRUCTOR</td><td></td><td>AM</td><td>PM</td><td></td><td></td><td></td></tr>
<tr><td>☐ EMPLOYEE
☐ CONTRUCTOR</td><td></td><td>AM</td><td>PM</td><td></td><td></td><td></td></tr>
<tr><td>☐ EMPLOYEE
☐ CONTRUCTOR</td><td></td><td>AM</td><td>PM</td><td></td><td></td><td></td></tr>
<tr><td>☐ EMPLOYEE
☐ CONTRUCTOR</td><td></td><td>AM</td><td>PM</td><td></td><td></td><td></td></tr>
<tr><td>☐ EMPLOYEE
☐ CONTRUCTOR</td><td></td><td>AM</td><td>PM</td><td></td><td></td><td></td></tr>
<tr><td>☐ EMPLOYEE
☐ CONTRUCTOR</td><td></td><td>AM</td><td>PM</td><td></td><td></td><td></td></tr>
<tr><td>☐ EMPLOYEE
☐ CONTRUCTOR</td><td></td><td>AM</td><td>PM</td><td></td><td></td><td></td></tr>
</table>

EQUIPMENT ON SITE	NO. OF UNITE	WORKING YES / NO

HIRED EQUIPMENT	NO. OF UNITE	EQUIPMENT RENTED	FROM	RATE

NAME: _______________________ SIGNATURE: _______________________

MO   TU   WE   TH   FR   SA   SU
☐   ☐   ☐   ☐   ☐   ☐   ☐

DATE: /   /

PROJECT:

FOREMAN:

WEATHER

F°______   C°______   ______ AM   ______ PM

| HOURS DUE TO BAD WEATHER | ISSUED AND DELAYS |

NOTE: ____

COMPLETION DATE	DAYS AHEAD OF SCHEDULE	DAYS BEHIND SCHEDULE

SAFETY AND INCIDENTS

SAFETY ISSUES THAT NEED TO BE ADDRESSED	ACCIDENTS / INCIDENTS / STEPS NEEDED TO RESOLVE

SUMMARY OF THE WORK DONE TODAY

IMPORTANT NOTES

NAME	SIGNATURE

TODAY LABOR							
INITIALS	TRADE	START	FINISH	PAID HOURS	OVERTIME	COMPANY
☐ EMPLOYEE ☐ CONTRUCTOR		AM	PM			
☐ EMPLOYEE ☐ CONTRUCTOR		AM	PM			
☐ EMPLOYEE ☐ CONTRUCTOR		AM	PM			
☐ EMPLOYEE ☐ CONTRUCTOR		AM	PM			
☐ EMPLOYEE ☐ CONTRUCTOR		AM	PM			
☐ EMPLOYEE ☐ CONTRUCTOR		AM	PM			
☐ EMPLOYEE ☐ CONTRUCTOR		AM	PM			
☐ EMPLOYEE ☐ CONTRUCTOR		AM	PM			

EQUIPMENT ON SITE	NO. OF UNITE	WORKING YES / NO

HIRED EQUIPMENT	NO. OF UNITE	EQUIPMENT RENTED	FROM	RATE

NAME: _______________________   SIGNATURE: _______________________

MO TU WE TH FR SA SU
☐   ☐   ☐   ☐   ☐   ☐   ☐

DATE: /   /

PROJECT:

FOREMAN:

WEATHER

F°_____ C°_____   _____AM _____PM

HOURS DUE TO BAD WEATHER	ISSUED AND DELAYS

NOTE: ____

COMPLETION DATE	DAYS AHEAD OF SCHEDULE	DAYS BEHIND SCHEDULE

SAFETY AND INCIDENTS

SAFETY ISSUES THAT NEED TO BE ADDRESSED	ACCIDENTS / INCIDENTS / STEPS NEEDED TO RESOLVE

SUMMARY OF THE WORK DONE TODAY

IMPORTANT NOTES

NAME	SIGNATURE

TODAY LABOR

INITIALS	TRADE	START	FINISH	PAID HOURS	OVERTIME	COMPANY
☐ EMPLOYEE ☐ CONTRUCTOR		AM	PM			
☐ EMPLOYEE ☐ CONTRUCTOR		AM	PM			
☐ EMPLOYEE ☐ CONTRUCTOR		AM	PM			
☐ EMPLOYEE ☐ CONTRUCTOR		AM	PM			
☐ EMPLOYEE ☐ CONTRUCTOR		AM	PM			
☐ EMPLOYEE ☐ CONTRUCTOR		AM	PM			
☐ EMPLOYEE ☐ CONTRUCTOR		AM	PM			
☐ EMPLOYEE ☐ CONTRUCTOR		AM	PM			

EQUIPMENT ON SITE	NO. OF UNITE	WORKING YES / NO

HIRED EQUIPMENT	NO. OF UNITE	EQUIPMENT RENTED	FROM	RATE

NAME: _______________________   SIGNATURE: _______________________

MO TU WE TH FR SA SU

DATE: ___ / ___ / ___

PROJECT:

FOREMAN:

WEATHER

F° ___ C° ___ ___ AM ___ PM

HOURS DUE TO BAD WEATHER

ISSUED AND DELAYS

NOTE:

COMPLETION DATE	DAYS AHEAD OF SCHEDULE	DAYS BEHIND SCHEDULE

SAFETY AND INCIDENTS

SAFETY ISSUES THAT NEED TO BE ADDRESSED	ACCIDENTS / INCIDENTS / STEPS NEEDED TO RESOLVE

SUMMARY OF THE WORK DONE TODAY

IMPORTANT NOTES

NAME	SIGNATURE

TODAY LABOR

INITIALS	TRADE	START	FINISH	PAID HOURS	OVERTIME	COMPANY
☐ EMPLOYEE ☐ CONTRUCTOR		AM	PM			
☐ EMPLOYEE ☐ CONTRUCTOR		AM	PM			
☐ EMPLOYEE ☐ CONTRUCTOR		AM	PM			
☐ EMPLOYEE ☐ CONTRUCTOR		AM	PM			
☐ EMPLOYEE ☐ CONTRUCTOR		AM	PM			
☐ EMPLOYEE ☐ CONTRUCTOR		AM	PM			
☐ EMPLOYEE ☐ CONTRUCTOR		AM	PM			
☐ EMPLOYEE ☐ CONTRUCTOR		AM	PM			

EQUIPMENT ON SITE	NO. OF UNITE	WORKING YES / NO

HIRED EQUIPMENT	NO. OF UNITE	EQUIPMENT RENTED	FROM	RATE

NAME: _______________________   SIGNATURE: _______________________

MO   TU   WE   TH   FR   SA   SU
☐   ☐   ☐   ☐   ☐   ☐   ☐

DATE: /   /

PROJECT:

FOREMAN:

WEATHER

F°_____ C°_____   _____ AM   _____ PM

HOURS DUE TO BAD WEATHER

ISSUED AND DELAYS

NOTE: ____

COMPLETION DATE	DAYS AHEAD OF SCHEDULE	DAYS BEHIND SCHEDULE

SAFETY AND INCIDENTS

SAFETY ISSUES THAT NEED TO BE ADDRESSED	ACCIDENTS / INCIDENTS / STEPS NEEDED TO RESOLVE

SUMMARY OF THE WORK DONE TODAY

IMPORTANT NOTES

NAME	SIGNATURE

TODAY LABOR

INITIALS	TRADE	START	FINISH	PAID HOURS	OVERTIME	COMPANY
☐ EMPLOYEE ☐ CONTRUCTOR		AM	PM			
☐ EMPLOYEE ☐ CONTRUCTOR		AM	PM			
☐ EMPLOYEE ☐ CONTRUCTOR		AM	PM			
☐ EMPLOYEE ☐ CONTRUCTOR		AM	PM			
☐ EMPLOYEE ☐ CONTRUCTOR		AM	PM			
☐ EMPLOYEE ☐ CONTRUCTOR		AM	PM			
☐ EMPLOYEE ☐ CONTRUCTOR		AM	PM			
☐ EMPLOYEE ☐ CONTRUCTOR		AM	PM			

EQUIPMENT ON SITE	NO. OF UNITE	WORKING YES / NO

HIRED EQUIPMENT	NO. OF UNITE	EQUIPMENT RENTED	FROM	RATE

NAME: _______________________   SIGNATURE: _______________________

MO   TU   WE   TH   FR   SA   SU

DATE: / /

PROJECT:

FOREMAN:

WEATHER

F° _____ C° _____   _____ AM   _____ PM

HOURS DUE TO BAD WEATHER

ISSUED AND DELAYS

NOTE: _____________________________

COMPLETION DATE	DAYS AHEAD OF SCHEDULE	DAYS BEHIND SCHEDULE

SAFETY AND INCIDENTS

SAFETY ISSUES THAT NEED TO BE ADDRESSED	ACCIDENTS / INCIDENTS / STEPS NEEDED TO RESOLVE

SUMMARY OF THE WORK DONE TODAY

IMPORTANT NOTES

NAME	SIGNATURE

TODAY LABOR

INITIALS	TRADE	START	FINISH	PAID HOURS	OVERTIME	COMPANY
☐ EMPLOYEE ☐ CONTRUCTOR		AM	PM			
☐ EMPLOYEE ☐ CONTRUCTOR		AM	PM			
☐ EMPLOYEE ☐ CONTRUCTOR		AM	PM			
☐ EMPLOYEE ☐ CONTRUCTOR		AM	PM			
☐ EMPLOYEE ☐ CONTRUCTOR		AM	PM			
☐ EMPLOYEE ☐ CONTRUCTOR		AM	PM			
☐ EMPLOYEE ☐ CONTRUCTOR		AM	PM			
☐ EMPLOYEE ☐ CONTRUCTOR		AM	PM			

EQUIPMENT ON SITE	NO. OF UNITE	WORKING YES / NO

HIRED EQUIPMENT	NO. OF UNITE	EQUIPMENT RENTED	FROM	RATE

NAME: ______________________   SIGNATURE: ______________________

MO TU WE TH FR SA SU
☐   ☐   ☐   ☐   ☐   ☐   ☐

DATE: /   /

PROJECT:

FOREMAN:

WEATHER

F°______ C°______   ______ AM   ______ PM

HOURS DUE TO BAD WEATHER	ISSUED AND DELAYS

NOTE: ____

COMPLETION DATE	DAYS AHEAD OF SCHEDULE	DAYS BEHIND SCHEDULE

SAFETY AND INCIDENTS

SAFETY ISSUES THAT NEED TO BE ADDRESSED	ACCIDENTS / INCIDENTS / STEPS NEEDED TO RESOLVE

SUMMARY OF THE WORK DONE TODAY

IMPORTANT NOTES

NAME	SIGNATURE

TODAY LABOR

INITIALS	TRADE	START	FINISH	PAID HOURS	OVERTIME	COMPANY
☐ EMPLOYEE ☐ CONTRUCTOR		AM	PM			
☐ EMPLOYEE ☐ CONTRUCTOR		AM	PM			
☐ EMPLOYEE ☐ CONTRUCTOR		AM	PM			
☐ EMPLOYEE ☐ CONTRUCTOR		AM	PM			
☐ EMPLOYEE ☐ CONTRUCTOR		AM	PM			
☐ EMPLOYEE ☐ CONTRUCTOR		AM	PM			
☐ EMPLOYEE ☐ CONTRUCTOR		AM	PM			
☐ EMPLOYEE ☐ CONTRUCTOR		AM	PM			

EQUIPMENT ON SITE	NO. OF UNITE	WORKING YES / NO

HIRED EQUIPMENT	NO. OF UNITE	EQUIPMENT RENTED	FROM	RATE

NAME: _____________________________   SIGNATURE: _____________________________

MO TU WE TH FR SA SU
☐ ☐ ☐ ☐ ☐ ☐ ☐

DATE: /   /

PROJECT:

FOREMAN:

WEATHER

F° _______ C° _______   _______ AM _______ PM

HOURS DUE TO BAD WEATHER

ISSUED AND DELAYS

NOTE: ____

COMPLETION DATE	DAYS AHEAD OF SCHEDULE	DAYS BEHIND SCHEDULE

SAFETY AND INCIDENTS

SAFETY ISSUES THAT NEED TO BE ADDRESSED	ACCIDENTS / INCIDENTS / STEPS NEEDED TO RESOLVE

SUMMARY OF THE WORK DONE TODAY

IMPORTANT NOTES

NAME	SIGNATURE

TODAY LABOR

INITIALS	TRADE	START	FINISH	PAID HOURS	OVERTIME	COMPANY
☐ EMPLOYEE ☐ CONTRUCTOR		AM	PM			
☐ EMPLOYEE ☐ CONTRUCTOR		AM	PM			
☐ EMPLOYEE ☐ CONTRUCTOR		AM	PM			
☐ EMPLOYEE ☐ CONTRUCTOR		AM	PM			
☐ EMPLOYEE ☐ CONTRUCTOR		AM	PM			
☐ EMPLOYEE ☐ CONTRUCTOR		AM	PM			
☐ EMPLOYEE ☐ CONTRUCTOR		AM	PM			
☐ EMPLOYEE ☐ CONTRUCTOR		AM	PM			

EQUIPMENT ON SITE	NO. OF UNITE	WORKING YES / NO

HIRED EQUIPMENT	NO. OF UNITE	EQUIPMENT RENTED	FROM	RATE

NAME: _______________________   SIGNATURE: _______________________

MO TU WE TH FR SA SU
☐   ☐   ☐   ☐   ☐   ☐   ☐

DATE: / /

PROJECT:

FOREMAN:

WEATHER

F°_____ C°_____   _____ AM   _____ PM

HOURS DUE TO BAD WEATHER

ISSUED AND DELAYS

NOTE: ____

COMPLETION DATE	DAYS AHEAD OF SCHEDULE	DAYS BEHIND SCHEDULE

SAFETY AND INCIDENTS

SAFETY ISSUES THAT NEED TO BE ADDRESSED	ACCIDENTS / INCIDENTS / STEPS NEEDED TO RESOLVE

SUMMARY OF THE WORK DONE TODAY

IMPORTANT NOTES

NAME	SIGNATURE

<table>
<tr><td colspan="7" align="center">TODAY LABOR</td></tr>
<tr><td>INITIALS</td><td>TRADE</td><td>START</td><td>FINISH</td><td>PAID HOURS</td><td>OVERTIME</td><td>COMPANY</td></tr>
<tr><td>☐ EMPLOYEE
☐ CONTRUCTOR</td><td></td><td>AM</td><td>PM</td><td></td><td></td><td></td></tr>
<tr><td>☐ EMPLOYEE
☐ CONTRUCTOR</td><td></td><td>AM</td><td>PM</td><td></td><td></td><td></td></tr>
<tr><td>☐ EMPLOYEE
☐ CONTRUCTOR</td><td></td><td>AM</td><td>PM</td><td></td><td></td><td></td></tr>
<tr><td>☐ EMPLOYEE
☐ CONTRUCTOR</td><td></td><td>AM</td><td>PM</td><td></td><td></td><td></td></tr>
<tr><td>☐ EMPLOYEE
☐ CONTRUCTOR</td><td></td><td>AM</td><td>PM</td><td></td><td></td><td></td></tr>
<tr><td>☐ EMPLOYEE
☐ CONTRUCTOR</td><td></td><td>AM</td><td>PM</td><td></td><td></td><td></td></tr>
<tr><td>☐ EMPLOYEE
☐ CONTRUCTOR</td><td></td><td>AM</td><td>PM</td><td></td><td></td><td></td></tr>
<tr><td>☐ EMPLOYEE
☐ CONTRUCTOR</td><td></td><td>AM</td><td>PM</td><td></td><td></td><td></td></tr>
</table>

EQUIPMENT ON SITE	NO. OF UNITE	WORKING YES / NO

HIRED EQUIPMENT	NO. OF UNITE	EQUIPMENT RENTED	FROM	RATE

NAME: _______________________   SIGNATURE: _______________________

MO   TU   WE   TH   FR   SA   SU
☐   ☐   ☐   ☐   ☐   ☐   ☐

DATE: /   /

PROJECT:

FOREMAN:

WEATHER

F°______   C°______   ______ AM   ______ PM

HOURS DUE TO BAD WEATHER

ISSUED AND DELAYS

NOTE: ____

COMPLETION DATE	DAYS AHEAD OF SCHEDULE	DAYS BEHIND SCHEDULE

SAFETY AND INCIDENTS

SAFETY ISSUES THAT NEED TO BE ADDRESSED	ACCIDENTS / INCIDENTS / STEPS NEEDED TO RESOLVE

SUMMARY OF THE WORK DONE TODAY

IMPORTANT NOTES

NAME	SIGNATURE

TODAY LABOR

INITIALS	TRADE	START	FINISH	PAID HOURS	OVERTIME	COMPANY
☐ EMPLOYEE ☐ CONTRUCTOR		AM	PM			
☐ EMPLOYEE ☐ CONTRUCTOR		AM	PM			
☐ EMPLOYEE ☐ CONTRUCTOR		AM	PM			
☐ EMPLOYEE ☐ CONTRUCTOR		AM	PM			
☐ EMPLOYEE ☐ CONTRUCTOR		AM	PM			
☐ EMPLOYEE ☐ CONTRUCTOR		AM	PM			
☐ EMPLOYEE ☐ CONTRUCTOR		AM	PM			
☐ EMPLOYEE ☐ CONTRUCTOR		AM	PM			

EQUIPMENT ON SITE	NO. OF UNITE	WORKING YES / NO

HIRED EQUIPMENT	NO. OF UNITE	EQUIPMENT RENTED	FROM	RATE

NAME: _________________________   SIGNATURE: _________________________

MO   TU   WE   TH   FR   SA   SU
☐   ☐   ☐   ☐   ☐   ☐   ☐

DATE: /   /

PROJECT:

FOREMAN:

WEATHER

F°_____ C°_____   _____ AM   _____ PM

HOURS DUE TO BAD WEATHER	ISSUED AND DELAYS

NOTE: ____

COMPLETION DATE	DAYS AHEAD OF SCHEDULE	DAYS BEHIND SCHEDULE

SAFETY AND INCIDENTS

SAFETY ISSUES THAT NEED TO BE ADDRESSED	ACCIDENTS / INCIDENTS / STEPS NEEDED TO RESOLVE

SUMMARY OF THE WORK DONE TODAY

IMPORTANT NOTES

NAME	SIGNATURE

TODAY LABOR

INITIALS	TRADE	START	FINISH	PAID HOURS	OVERTIME	COMPANY
☐ EMPLOYEE ☐ CONTRUCTOR		AM	PM			
☐ EMPLOYEE ☐ CONTRUCTOR		AM	PM			
☐ EMPLOYEE ☐ CONTRUCTOR		AM	PM			
☐ EMPLOYEE ☐ CONTRUCTOR		AM	PM			
☐ EMPLOYEE ☐ CONTRUCTOR		AM	PM			
☐ EMPLOYEE ☐ CONTRUCTOR		AM	PM			
☐ EMPLOYEE ☐ CONTRUCTOR		AM	PM			
☐ EMPLOYEE ☐ CONTRUCTOR		AM	PM			

EQUIPMENT ON SITE	NO. OF UNITE	WORKING YES / NO

HIRED EQUIPMENT	NO. OF UNITE	EQUIPMENT RENTED	FROM	RATE

NAME: _______________________   SIGNATURE: _______________________

MO TU WE TH FR SA SU
☐   ☐   ☐   ☐   ☐   ☐   ☐

DATE: ___ / ___ / ___

PROJECT:

FOREMAN:

WEATHER

F° _______ C° _______ _______ AM _______ PM

HOURS DUE TO BAD WEATHER

ISSUED AND DELAYS

NOTE: _______________________________________

COMPLETION DATE	DAYS AHEAD OF SCHEDULE	DAYS BEHIND SCHEDULE

SAFETY AND INCIDENTS

SAFETY ISSUES THAT NEED TO BE ADDRESSED	ACCIDENTS / INCIDENTS / STEPS NEEDED TO RESOLVE

SUMMARY OF THE WORK DONE TODAY

IMPORTANT NOTES

NAME	SIGNATURE

TODAY LABOR						
INITIALS	TRADE	START	FINISH	PAID HOURS	OVERTIME	COMPANY
☐ EMPLOYEE ☐ CONTRUCTOR		AM	PM			
☐ EMPLOYEE ☐ CONTRUCTOR		AM	PM			
☐ EMPLOYEE ☐ CONTRUCTOR		AM	PM			
☐ EMPLOYEE ☐ CONTRUCTOR		AM	PM			
☐ EMPLOYEE ☐ CONTRUCTOR		AM	PM			
☐ EMPLOYEE ☐ CONTRUCTOR		AM	PM			
☐ EMPLOYEE ☐ CONTRUCTOR		AM	PM			
☐ EMPLOYEE ☐ CONTRUCTOR		AM	PM			

EQUIPMENT ON SITE	NO. OF UNITE	WORKING YES / NO

HIRED EQUIPMENT	NO. OF UNITE	EQUIPMENT RENTED	FROM	RATE

NAME: ________________________   SIGNATURE: ________________________

MO	TU	WE	TH	FR	SA	SU	DATE: / /
☐	☐	☐	☐	☐	☐	☐	

PROJECT:

FOREMAN:

WEATHER F°_____ C°_____ _____ AM _____ PM

HOURS DUE TO BAD WEATHER	ISSUED AND DELAYS

NOTE: ____

COMPLETION DATE	DAYS AHEAD OF SCHEDULE	DAYS BEHIND SCHEDULE

SAFETY AND INCIDENTS

SAFETY ISSUES THAT NEED TO BE ADDRESSED	ACCIDENTS / INCIDENTS / STEPS NEEDED TO RESOLVE

SUMMARY OF THE WORK DONE TODAY

IMPORTANT NOTES

NAME	SIGNATURE

TODAY LABOR

INITIALS	TRADE	START	FINISH	PAID HOURS	OVERTIME	COMPANY
☐ EMPLOYEE ☐ CONTRUCTOR		AM	PM			
☐ EMPLOYEE ☐ CONTRUCTOR		AM	PM			
☐ EMPLOYEE ☐ CONTRUCTOR		AM	PM			
☐ EMPLOYEE ☐ CONTRUCTOR		AM	PM			
☐ EMPLOYEE ☐ CONTRUCTOR		AM	PM			
☐ EMPLOYEE ☐ CONTRUCTOR		AM	PM			
☐ EMPLOYEE ☐ CONTRUCTOR		AM	PM			
☐ EMPLOYEE ☐ CONTRUCTOR		AM	PM			

EQUIPMENT ON SITE	NO. OF UNITE	WORKING YES / NO

HIRED EQUIPMENT	NO. OF UNITE	EQUIPMENT RENTED	FROM	RATE

NAME: _______________________   SIGNATURE: _______________________

MO   TU   WE   TH   FR   SA   SU
☐   ☐   ☐   ☐   ☐   ☐   ☐

DATE: /   /

PROJECT:

FOREMAN:

WEATHER

F°_____ C°_____   _____ AM _____ PM

HOURS DUE TO BAD WEATHER	ISSUED AND DELAYS

NOTE: _____________________________________

COMPLETION DATE	DAYS AHEAD OF SCHEDULE	DAYS BEHIND SCHEDULE

SAFETY AND INCIDENTS

SAFETY ISSUES THAT NEED TO BE ADDRESSED	ACCIDENTS / INCIDENTS / STEPS NEEDED TO RESOLVE

SUMMARY OF THE WORK DONE TODAY

IMPORTANT NOTES

NAME	SIGNATURE

TODAY LABOR

INITIALS	TRADE	START	FINISH	PAID HOURS	OVERTIME	COMPANY
☐ EMPLOYEE ☐ CONTRUCTOR		AM	PM			
☐ EMPLOYEE ☐ CONTRUCTOR		AM	PM			
☐ EMPLOYEE ☐ CONTRUCTOR		AM	PM			
☐ EMPLOYEE ☐ CONTRUCTOR		AM	PM			
☐ EMPLOYEE ☐ CONTRUCTOR		AM	PM			
☐ EMPLOYEE ☐ CONTRUCTOR		AM	PM			
☐ EMPLOYEE ☐ CONTRUCTOR		AM	PM			
☐ EMPLOYEE ☐ CONTRUCTOR		AM	PM			

EQUIPMENT ON SITE	NO. OF UNITE	WORKING YES / NO

HIRED EQUIPMENT	NO. OF UNITE	EQUIPMENT RENTED	FROM	RATE

NAME: _______________________   SIGNATURE: _______________________

MO TU WE TH FR SA SU
☐   ☐   ☐   ☐   ☐   ☐   ☐

DATE: /   /

PROJECT:

FOREMAN:

WEATHER

F°_____ C°_____   _____ AM   _____ PM

HOURS DUE TO BAD WEATHER

ISSUED AND DELAYS

NOTE: ____

COMPLETION DATE	DAYS AHEAD OF SCHEDULE	DAYS BEHIND SCHEDULE

SAFETY AND INCIDENTS

SAFETY ISSUES THAT NEED TO BE ADDRESSED	ACCIDENTS / INCIDENTS / STEPS NEEDED TO RESOLVE

SUMMARY OF THE WORK DONE TODAY

IMPORTANT NOTES

NAME	SIGNATURE

<table>
<tr><th colspan="8">TODAY LABOR</th></tr>
<tr><th>INITIALS</th><th>TRADE</th><th>START</th><th>FINISH</th><th>PAID HOURS</th><th>OVERTIME</th><th>COMPANY</th></tr>
<tr><td>☐ EMPLOYEE
☐ CONTRUCTOR</td><td></td><td>AM</td><td>PM</td><td></td><td></td><td></td></tr>
<tr><td>☐ EMPLOYEE
☐ CONTRUCTOR</td><td></td><td>AM</td><td>PM</td><td></td><td></td><td></td></tr>
<tr><td>☐ EMPLOYEE
☐ CONTRUCTOR</td><td></td><td>AM</td><td>PM</td><td></td><td></td><td></td></tr>
<tr><td>☐ EMPLOYEE
☐ CONTRUCTOR</td><td></td><td>AM</td><td>PM</td><td></td><td></td><td></td></tr>
<tr><td>☐ EMPLOYEE
☐ CONTRUCTOR</td><td></td><td>AM</td><td>PM</td><td></td><td></td><td></td></tr>
<tr><td>☐ EMPLOYEE
☐ CONTRUCTOR</td><td></td><td>AM</td><td>PM</td><td></td><td></td><td></td></tr>
<tr><td>☐ EMPLOYEE
☐ CONTRUCTOR</td><td></td><td>AM</td><td>PM</td><td></td><td></td><td></td></tr>
<tr><td>☐ EMPLOYEE
☐ CONTRUCTOR</td><td></td><td>AM</td><td>PM</td><td></td><td></td><td></td></tr>
</table>

EQUIPMENT ON SITE	NO. OF UNITE	WORKING YES / NO

HIRED EQUIPMENT	NO. OF UNITE	EQUIPMENT RENTED	FROM	RATE

NAME: _______________________   SIGNATURE: _______________________

MO TU WE TH FR SA SU
☐   ☐   ☐   ☐   ☐   ☐   ☐

DATE: /   /

PROJECT:

FOREMAN:

WEATHER

F° _____ C° _____   _____ AM   _____ PM

HOURS DUE TO BAD WEATHER

ISSUED AND DELAYS

NOTE: _______________

COMPLETION DATE	DAYS AHEAD OF SCHEDULE	DAYS BEHIND SCHEDULE

SAFETY AND INCIDENTS

SAFETY ISSUES THAT NEED TO BE ADDRESSED	ACCIDENTS / INCIDENTS / STEPS NEEDED TO RESOLVE

SUMMARY OF THE WORK DONE TODAY

IMPORTANT NOTES

NAME	SIGNATURE

TODAY LABOR

INITIALS	TRADE	START	FINISH	PAID HOURS	OVERTIME	COMPANY
☐ EMPLOYEE ☐ CONTRUCTOR		AM	PM			
☐ EMPLOYEE ☐ CONTRUCTOR		AM	PM			
☐ EMPLOYEE ☐ CONTRUCTOR		AM	PM			
☐ EMPLOYEE ☐ CONTRUCTOR		AM	PM			
☐ EMPLOYEE ☐ CONTRUCTOR		AM	PM			
☐ EMPLOYEE ☐ CONTRUCTOR		AM	PM			
☐ EMPLOYEE ☐ CONTRUCTOR		AM	PM			
☐ EMPLOYEE ☐ CONTRUCTOR		AM	PM			

EQUIPMENT ON SITE	NO. OF UNITE	WORKING YES / NO

HIRED EQUIPMENT	NO. OF UNITE	EQUIPMENT RENTED	FROM	RATE

NAME: ___________________________   SIGNATURE: ___________________________

MO   TU   WE   TH   FR   SA   SU
☐   ☐   ☐   ☐   ☐   ☐   ☐

DATE: /   /

PROJECT:

FOREMAN:

WEATHER

F°_____ C°_____   _____ AM   _____ PM

HOURS DUE TO BAD WEATHER

ISSUED AND DELAYS

NOTE: ____

COMPLETION DATE	DAYS AHEAD OF SCHEDULE	DAYS BEHIND SCHEDULE

SAFETY AND INCIDENTS

SAFETY ISSUES THAT NEED TO BE ADDRESSED	ACCIDENTS / INCIDENTS / STEPS NEEDED TO RESOLVE

SUMMARY OF THE WORK DONE TODAY

IMPORTANT NOTES

NAME	SIGNATURE

TODAY LABOR

INITIALS	TRADE	START	FINISH	PAID HOURS	OVERTIME	COMPANY
☐ EMPLOYEE ☐ CONTRUCTOR		AM	PM			
☐ EMPLOYEE ☐ CONTRUCTOR		AM	PM			
☐ EMPLOYEE ☐ CONTRUCTOR		AM	PM			
☐ EMPLOYEE ☐ CONTRUCTOR		AM	PM			
☐ EMPLOYEE ☐ CONTRUCTOR		AM	PM			
☐ EMPLOYEE ☐ CONTRUCTOR		AM	PM			
☐ EMPLOYEE ☐ CONTRUCTOR		AM	PM			
☐ EMPLOYEE ☐ CONTRUCTOR		AM	PM			

EQUIPMENT ON SITE	NO. OF UNITE	WORKING YES / NO

HIRED EQUIPMENT	NO. OF UNITE	EQUIPMENT RENTED	FROM	RATE

NAME: _______________________   SIGNATURE: _______________________

MO TU WE TH FR SA SU
☐   ☐   ☐   ☐   ☐   ☐   ☐

DATE: ___ / ___ / ___

PROJECT:

FOREMAN:

WEATHER

F° _____ C° _____ _____ AM _____ PM

HOURS DUE TO BAD WEATHER

ISSUED AND DELAYS

NOTE: _______________________________

COMPLETION DATE	DAYS AHEAD OF SCHEDULE	DAYS BEHIND SCHEDULE

SAFETY AND INCIDENTS

SAFETY ISSUES THAT NEED TO BE ADDRESSED	ACCIDENTS / INCIDENTS / STEPS NEEDED TO RESOLVE

SUMMARY OF THE WORK DONE TODAY

IMPORTANT NOTES

NAME	SIGNATURE

<table>
<tr><th colspan="7" align="center">TODAY LABOR</th></tr>
<tr><th>INITIALS</th><th>TRADE</th><th>START</th><th>FINISH</th><th>PAID HOURS</th><th>OVERTIME</th><th>COMPANY</th></tr>
<tr><td>☐ EMPLOYEE
☐ CONTRUCTOR</td><td></td><td>AM</td><td>PM</td><td></td><td></td><td></td></tr>
<tr><td>☐ EMPLOYEE
☐ CONTRUCTOR</td><td></td><td>AM</td><td>PM</td><td></td><td></td><td></td></tr>
<tr><td>☐ EMPLOYEE
☐ CONTRUCTOR</td><td></td><td>AM</td><td>PM</td><td></td><td></td><td></td></tr>
<tr><td>☐ EMPLOYEE
☐ CONTRUCTOR</td><td></td><td>AM</td><td>PM</td><td></td><td></td><td></td></tr>
<tr><td>☐ EMPLOYEE
☐ CONTRUCTOR</td><td></td><td>AM</td><td>PM</td><td></td><td></td><td></td></tr>
<tr><td>☐ EMPLOYEE
☐ CONTRUCTOR</td><td></td><td>AM</td><td>PM</td><td></td><td></td><td></td></tr>
<tr><td>☐ EMPLOYEE
☐ CONTRUCTOR</td><td></td><td>AM</td><td>PM</td><td></td><td></td><td></td></tr>
<tr><td>☐ EMPLOYEE
☐ CONTRUCTOR</td><td></td><td>AM</td><td>PM</td><td></td><td></td><td></td></tr>
</table>

EQUIPMENT ON SITE	NO. OF UNITE	WORKING YES / NO

HIRED EQUIPMENT	NO. OF UNITE	EQUIPMENT RENTED	FROM	RATE

NAME: _______________________   SIGNATURE: _______________________

MO TU WE TH FR SA SU
☐   ☐   ☐   ☐   ☐   ☐   ☐

DATE: ___ / ___ / ___

PROJECT:

FOREMAN:

WEATHER

F° _____ C° _____   _____ AM   _____ PM

HOURS DUE TO BAD WEATHER

ISSUED AND DELAYS

NOTE: _______________

COMPLETION DATE	DAYS AHEAD OF SCHEDULE	DAYS BEHIND SCHEDULE

SAFETY AND INCIDENTS

SAFETY ISSUES THAT NEED TO BE ADDRESSED	ACCIDENTS / INCIDENTS / STEPS NEEDED TO RESOLVE

SUMMARY OF THE WORK DONE TODAY

IMPORTANT NOTES

NAME	SIGNATURE

TODAY LABOR

INITIALS	TRADE	START	FINISH	PAID HOURS	OVERTIME	COMPANY
☐ EMPLOYEE ☐ CONTRUCTOR		AM	PM			
☐ EMPLOYEE ☐ CONTRUCTOR		AM	PM			
☐ EMPLOYEE ☐ CONTRUCTOR		AM	PM			
☐ EMPLOYEE ☐ CONTRUCTOR		AM	PM			
☐ EMPLOYEE ☐ CONTRUCTOR		AM	PM			
☐ EMPLOYEE ☐ CONTRUCTOR		AM	PM			
☐ EMPLOYEE ☐ CONTRUCTOR		AM	PM			
☐ EMPLOYEE ☐ CONTRUCTOR		AM	PM			

EQUIPMENT ON SITE	NO. OF UNITE	WORKING YES / NO

HIRED EQUIPMENT	NO. OF UNITE	EQUIPMENT RENTED	FROM	RATE

NAME: _______________________   SIGNATURE: _______________________

MO TU WE TH FR SA SU
☐   ☐   ☐   ☐   ☐   ☐   ☐

DATE: /   /

PROJECT:

FOREMAN:

WEATHER

F°_____ C°_____ _____ AM _____ PM

HOURS DUE TO BAD WEATHER

ISSUED AND DELAYS

NOTE: ____

COMPLETION DATE	DAYS AHEAD OF SCHEDULE	DAYS BEHIND SCHEDULE

SAFETY AND INCIDENTS

SAFETY ISSUES THAT NEED TO BE ADDRESSED	ACCIDENTS / INCIDENTS / STEPS NEEDED TO RESOLVE

SUMMARY OF THE WORK DONE TODAY

IMPORTANT NOTES

NAME	SIGNATURE

<table>
<tr><th colspan="8" style="text-align:center">TODAY LABOR</th></tr>
<tr><th>INITIALS</th><th>TRADE</th><th>START</th><th>FINISH</th><th>PAID HOURS</th><th>OVERTIME</th><th>COMPANY</th></tr>
<tr><td>☐ EMPLOYEE
☐ CONTRUCTOR</td><td></td><td>AM</td><td>PM</td><td></td><td></td><td></td></tr>
<tr><td>☐ EMPLOYEE
☐ CONTRUCTOR</td><td></td><td>AM</td><td>PM</td><td></td><td></td><td></td></tr>
<tr><td>☐ EMPLOYEE
☐ CONTRUCTOR</td><td></td><td>AM</td><td>PM</td><td></td><td></td><td></td></tr>
<tr><td>☐ EMPLOYEE
☐ CONTRUCTOR</td><td></td><td>AM</td><td>PM</td><td></td><td></td><td></td></tr>
<tr><td>☐ EMPLOYEE
☐ CONTRUCTOR</td><td></td><td>AM</td><td>PM</td><td></td><td></td><td></td></tr>
<tr><td>☐ EMPLOYEE
☐ CONTRUCTOR</td><td></td><td>AM</td><td>PM</td><td></td><td></td><td></td></tr>
<tr><td>☐ EMPLOYEE
☐ CONTRUCTOR</td><td></td><td>AM</td><td>PM</td><td></td><td></td><td></td></tr>
<tr><td>☐ EMPLOYEE
☐ CONTRUCTOR</td><td></td><td>AM</td><td>PM</td><td></td><td></td><td></td></tr>
</table>

EQUIPMENT ON SITE	NO. OF UNITE	WORKING YES / NO

HIRED EQUIPMENT	NO. OF UNITE	EQUIPMENT RENTED	FROM	RATE

NAME: ________________________________   SIGNATURE: ________________________________

MO TU WE TH FR SA SU
☐ ☐ ☐ ☐ ☐ ☐ ☐

DATE: / /

PROJECT:

FOREMAN:

WEATHER

F°_____ C°_____   _____ AM _____ PM

HOURS DUE TO BAD WEATHER

ISSUED AND DELAYS

NOTE: _______________________________

COMPLETION DATE	DAYS AHEAD OF SCHEDULE	DAYS BEHIND SCHEDULE

SAFETY AND INCIDENTS

SAFETY ISSUES THAT NEED TO BE ADDRESSED	ACCIDENTS / INCIDENTS / STEPS NEEDED TO RESOLVE

SUMMARY OF THE WORK DONE TODAY

IMPORTANT NOTES

NAME	SIGNATURE

<table>
<tr><td colspan="7" align="center">TODAY LABOR</td></tr>
<tr><td>INITIALS</td><td>TRADE</td><td>START</td><td>FINISH</td><td>PAID HOURS</td><td>OVERTIME</td><td>COMPANY</td></tr>
<tr><td>☐ EMPLOYEE
☐ CONTRUCTOR</td><td></td><td>AM</td><td>PM</td><td></td><td></td><td></td></tr>
<tr><td>☐ EMPLOYEE
☐ CONTRUCTOR</td><td></td><td>AM</td><td>PM</td><td></td><td></td><td></td></tr>
<tr><td>☐ EMPLOYEE
☐ CONTRUCTOR</td><td></td><td>AM</td><td>PM</td><td></td><td></td><td></td></tr>
<tr><td>☐ EMPLOYEE
☐ CONTRUCTOR</td><td></td><td>AM</td><td>PM</td><td></td><td></td><td></td></tr>
<tr><td>☐ EMPLOYEE
☐ CONTRUCTOR</td><td></td><td>AM</td><td>PM</td><td></td><td></td><td></td></tr>
<tr><td>☐ EMPLOYEE
☐ CONTRUCTOR</td><td></td><td>AM</td><td>PM</td><td></td><td></td><td></td></tr>
<tr><td>☐ EMPLOYEE
☐ CONTRUCTOR</td><td></td><td>AM</td><td>PM</td><td></td><td></td><td></td></tr>
<tr><td>☐ EMPLOYEE
☐ CONTRUCTOR</td><td></td><td>AM</td><td>PM</td><td></td><td></td><td></td></tr>
</table>

EQUIPMENT ON SITE	NO. OF UNITE	WORKING YES / NO

HIRED EQUIPMENT	NO. OF UNITE	EQUIPMENT RENTED	FROM	RATE

NAME: _______________________   SIGNATURE: _______________________

MO TU WE TH FR SA SU
☐   ☐   ☐   ☐   ☐   ☐   ☐

DATE: ___ / ___ / ___

PROJECT:

FOREMAN:

WEATHER F°____ C°____ ____ AM ____ PM

HOURS DUE TO BAD WEATHER

ISSUED AND DELAYS

NOTE: _______________

COMPLETION DATE	DAYS AHEAD OF SCHEDULE	DAYS BEHIND SCHEDULE

SAFETY AND INCIDENTS

SAFETY ISSUES THAT NEED TO BE ADDRESSED	ACCIDENTS / INCIDENTS / STEPS NEEDED TO RESOLVE

SUMMARY OF THE WORK DONE TODAY

IMPORTANT NOTES

NAME	SIGNATURE

<table>
<tr><td colspan="7" align="center">TODAY LABOR</td></tr>
<tr><td>INITIALS</td><td>TRADE</td><td>START</td><td>FINISH</td><td>PAID HOURS</td><td>OVERTIME</td><td>COMPANY</td></tr>
<tr><td>☐ EMPLOYEE
☐ CONTRUCTOR</td><td></td><td>AM</td><td>PM</td><td></td><td></td><td></td></tr>
<tr><td>☐ EMPLOYEE
☐ CONTRUCTOR</td><td></td><td>AM</td><td>PM</td><td></td><td></td><td></td></tr>
<tr><td>☐ EMPLOYEE
☐ CONTRUCTOR</td><td></td><td>AM</td><td>PM</td><td></td><td></td><td></td></tr>
<tr><td>☐ EMPLOYEE
☐ CONTRUCTOR</td><td></td><td>AM</td><td>PM</td><td></td><td></td><td></td></tr>
<tr><td>☐ EMPLOYEE
☐ CONTRUCTOR</td><td></td><td>AM</td><td>PM</td><td></td><td></td><td></td></tr>
<tr><td>☐ EMPLOYEE
☐ CONTRUCTOR</td><td></td><td>AM</td><td>PM</td><td></td><td></td><td></td></tr>
<tr><td>☐ EMPLOYEE
☐ CONTRUCTOR</td><td></td><td>AM</td><td>PM</td><td></td><td></td><td></td></tr>
<tr><td>☐ EMPLOYEE
☐ CONTRUCTOR</td><td></td><td>AM</td><td>PM</td><td></td><td></td><td></td></tr>
</table>

EQUIPMENT ON SITE	NO. OF UNITE	WORKING YES / NO

HIRED EQUIPMENT	NO. OF UNITE	EQUIPMENT RENTED	FROM	RATE

NAME: _______________   SIGNATURE: _______________

MO TU WE TH FR SA SU
☐   ☐   ☐   ☐   ☐   ☐   ☐

DATE: /   /

PROJECT:

FOREMAN:

WEATHER

F°_____ C°_____   _____ AM   _____ PM

HOURS DUE TO
BAD WEATHER

ISSUED AND DELAYS

NOTE: _______________________________________

COMPLETION DATE	DAYS AHEAD OF SCHEDULE	DAYS BEHIND SCHEDULE

SAFETY AND INCIDENTS

SAFETY ISSUES THAT NEED TO BE ADDRESSED	ACCIDENTS / INCIDENTS / STEPS NEEDED TO RESOLVE

SUMMARY OF THE WORK DONE TODAY

IMPORTANT NOTES

NAME	SIGNATURE

TODAY LABOR

INITIALS	TRADE	START	FINISH	PAID HOURS	OVERTIME	COMPANY
☐ EMPLOYEE ☐ CONTRUCTOR		AM	PM			
☐ EMPLOYEE ☐ CONTRUCTOR		AM	PM			
☐ EMPLOYEE ☐ CONTRUCTOR		AM	PM			
☐ EMPLOYEE ☐ CONTRUCTOR		AM	PM			
☐ EMPLOYEE ☐ CONTRUCTOR		AM	PM			
☐ EMPLOYEE ☐ CONTRUCTOR		AM	PM			
☐ EMPLOYEE ☐ CONTRUCTOR		AM	PM			
☐ EMPLOYEE ☐ CONTRUCTOR		AM	PM			

EQUIPMENT ON SITE	NO. OF UNITE	WORKING YES / NO

HIRED EQUIPMENT	NO. OF UNITE	EQUIPMENT RENTED	FROM	RATE

NAME: _______________________   SIGNATURE: _______________________

MO   TU   WE   TH   FR   SA   SU
☐   ☐   ☐   ☐   ☐   ☐   ☐

DATE: /   /

PROJECT:

FOREMAN:

WEATHER

F°_____   C°_____   _____ AM   _____ PM

HOURS DUE TO BAD WEATHER

ISSUED AND DELAYS

NOTE: ____

COMPLETION DATE	DAYS AHEAD OF SCHEDULE	DAYS BEHIND SCHEDULE

SAFETY AND INCIDENTS

SAFETY ISSUES THAT NEED TO BE ADDRESSED	ACCIDENTS / INCIDENTS / STEPS NEEDED TO RESOLVE

SUMMARY OF THE WORK DONE TODAY

IMPORTANT NOTES

NAME	SIGNATURE

TODAY LABOR

INITIALS	TRADE	START	FINISH	PAID HOURS	OVERTIME	COMPANY
☐ EMPLOYEE ☐ CONTRUCTOR		AM	PM			
☐ EMPLOYEE ☐ CONTRUCTOR		AM	PM			
☐ EMPLOYEE ☐ CONTRUCTOR		AM	PM			
☐ EMPLOYEE ☐ CONTRUCTOR		AM	PM			
☐ EMPLOYEE ☐ CONTRUCTOR		AM	PM			
☐ EMPLOYEE ☐ CONTRUCTOR		AM	PM			
☐ EMPLOYEE ☐ CONTRUCTOR		AM	PM			
☐ EMPLOYEE ☐ CONTRUCTOR		AM	PM			

EQUIPMENT ON SITE	NO. OF UNITE	WORKING YES / NO

HIRED EQUIPMENT	NO. OF UNITE	EQUIPMENT RENTED	FROM	RATE

NAME: _______________________   SIGNATURE: _______________________

MO TU WE TH FR SA SU
☐   ☐   ☐   ☐   ☐   ☐   ☐

DATE: /   /

PROJECT:

FOREMAN:

WEATHER

F°______ C°______   ______ AM   ______ PM

HOURS DUE TO BAD WEATHER	ISSUED AND DELAYS

NOTE: ____

COMPLETION DATE	DAYS AHEAD OF SCHEDULE	DAYS BEHIND SCHEDULE

SAFETY AND INCIDENTS

SAFETY ISSUES THAT NEED TO BE ADDRESSED	ACCIDENTS / INCIDENTS / STEPS NEEDED TO RESOLVE

SUMMARY OF THE WORK DONE TODAY

IMPORTANT NOTES

NAME	SIGNATURE

TODAY LABOR

INITIALS	TRADE	START	FINISH	PAID HOURS	OVERTIME	COMPANY
☐ EMPLOYEE ☐ CONTRUCTOR		AM	PM			
☐ EMPLOYEE ☐ CONTRUCTOR		AM	PM			
☐ EMPLOYEE ☐ CONTRUCTOR		AM	PM			
☐ EMPLOYEE ☐ CONTRUCTOR		AM	PM			
☐ EMPLOYEE ☐ CONTRUCTOR		AM	PM			
☐ EMPLOYEE ☐ CONTRUCTOR		AM	PM			
☐ EMPLOYEE ☐ CONTRUCTOR		AM	PM			
☐ EMPLOYEE ☐ CONTRUCTOR		AM	PM			

EQUIPMENT ON SITE	NO. OF UNITE	WORKING YES / NO

HIRED EQUIPMENT	NO. OF UNITE	EQUIPMENT RENTED	FROM	RATE

NAME: _______________________   SIGNATURE: _______________________

MO   TU   WE   TH   FR   SA   SU
☐   ☐   ☐   ☐   ☐   ☐   ☐

DATE: /   /

PROJECT:

FOREMAN:

WEATHER

F°_____   C°_____   _____ AM   _____ PM

HOURS DUE TO BAD WEATHER

ISSUED AND DELAYS

NOTE: ____

COMPLETION DATE	DAYS AHEAD OF SCHEDULE	DAYS BEHIND SCHEDULE

SAFETY AND INCIDENTS

SAFETY ISSUES THAT NEED TO BE ADDRESSED	ACCIDENTS / INCIDENTS / STEPS NEEDED TO RESOLVE

SUMMARY OF THE WORK DONE TODAY

IMPORTANT NOTES

NAME	SIGNATURE

TODAY LABOR

INITIALS	TRADE	START	FINISH	PAID HOURS	OVERTIME	COMPANY
☐ EMPLOYEE ☐ CONTRUCTOR		AM	PM			
☐ EMPLOYEE ☐ CONTRUCTOR		AM	PM			
☐ EMPLOYEE ☐ CONTRUCTOR		AM	PM			
☐ EMPLOYEE ☐ CONTRUCTOR		AM	PM			
☐ EMPLOYEE ☐ CONTRUCTOR		AM	PM			
☐ EMPLOYEE ☐ CONTRUCTOR		AM	PM			
☐ EMPLOYEE ☐ CONTRUCTOR		AM	PM			
☐ EMPLOYEE ☐ CONTRUCTOR		AM	PM			

EQUIPMENT ON SITE	NO. OF UNITE	WORKING YES / NO

HIRED EQUIPMENT	NO. OF UNITE	EQUIPMENT RENTED	FROM	RATE

NAME: _______________________________   SIGNATURE: _______________________________

MO ☐ TU ☐ WE ☐ TH ☐ FR ☐ SA ☐ SU ☐

DATE: ___ / ___ / ___

PROJECT:

FOREMAN:

WEATHER

F° _____ C° _____   _____ AM   _____ PM

HOURS DUE TO BAD WEATHER

ISSUED AND DELAYS

NOTE: ____

COMPLETION DATE	DAYS AHEAD OF SCHEDULE	DAYS BEHIND SCHEDULE

SAFETY AND INCIDENTS

SAFETY ISSUES THAT NEED TO BE ADDRESSED	ACCIDENTS / INCIDENTS / STEPS NEEDED TO RESOLVE

SUMMARY OF THE WORK DONE TODAY

IMPORTANT NOTES

NAME	SIGNATURE

TODAY LABOR

INITIALS	TRADE	START	FINISH	PAID HOURS	OVERTIME	COMPANY
☐ EMPLOYEE ☐ CONTRUCTOR		AM	PM			
☐ EMPLOYEE ☐ CONTRUCTOR		AM	PM			
☐ EMPLOYEE ☐ CONTRUCTOR		AM	PM			
☐ EMPLOYEE ☐ CONTRUCTOR		AM	PM			
☐ EMPLOYEE ☐ CONTRUCTOR		AM	PM			
☐ EMPLOYEE ☐ CONTRUCTOR		AM	PM			
☐ EMPLOYEE ☐ CONTRUCTOR		AM	PM			
☐ EMPLOYEE ☐ CONTRUCTOR		AM	PM			

EQUIPMENT ON SITE	NO. OF UNITE	WORKING YES / NO

HIRED EQUIPMENT	NO. OF UNITE	EQUIPMENT RENTED	FROM	RATE

NAME: ________________________   SIGNATURE: ________________________

MO TU WE TH FR SA SU
☐   ☐   ☐   ☐   ☐   ☐   ☐

DATE: ___ / ___ / ___

PROJECT:

FOREMAN:

WEATHER

F°_______ C°_______   _______ AM _______ PM

HOURS DUE TO BAD WEATHER	ISSUED AND DELAYS

NOTE: ____

COMPLETION DATE	DAYS AHEAD OF SCHEDULE	DAYS BEHIND SCHEDULE

SAFETY AND INCIDENTS

SAFETY ISSUES THAT NEED TO BE ADDRESSED	ACCIDENTS / INCIDENTS / STEPS NEEDED TO RESOLVE

SUMMARY OF THE WORK DONE TODAY

IMPORTANT NOTES

NAME	SIGNATURE

<table>
<tr><td colspan="7" align="center">TODAY LABOR</td></tr>
<tr><td>INITIALS</td><td>TRADE</td><td>START</td><td>FINISH</td><td>PAID HOURS</td><td>OVERTIME</td><td>COMPANY</td></tr>
<tr><td>☐ EMPLOYEE
☐ CONTRUCTOR</td><td></td><td>AM</td><td>PM</td><td></td><td></td><td></td></tr>
<tr><td>☐ EMPLOYEE
☐ CONTRUCTOR</td><td></td><td>AM</td><td>PM</td><td></td><td></td><td></td></tr>
<tr><td>☐ EMPLOYEE
☐ CONTRUCTOR</td><td></td><td>AM</td><td>PM</td><td></td><td></td><td></td></tr>
<tr><td>☐ EMPLOYEE
☐ CONTRUCTOR</td><td></td><td>AM</td><td>PM</td><td></td><td></td><td></td></tr>
<tr><td>☐ EMPLOYEE
☐ CONTRUCTOR</td><td></td><td>AM</td><td>PM</td><td></td><td></td><td></td></tr>
<tr><td>☐ EMPLOYEE
☐ CONTRUCTOR</td><td></td><td>AM</td><td>PM</td><td></td><td></td><td></td></tr>
<tr><td>☐ EMPLOYEE
☐ CONTRUCTOR</td><td></td><td>AM</td><td>PM</td><td></td><td></td><td></td></tr>
<tr><td>☐ EMPLOYEE
☐ CONTRUCTOR</td><td></td><td>AM</td><td>PM</td><td></td><td></td><td></td></tr>
</table>

EQUIPMENT ON SITE	NO. OF UNITE	WORKING YES / NO

HIRED EQUIPMENT	NO. OF UNITE	EQUIPMENT RENTED	FROM	RATE

NAME: _______________________   SIGNATURE: _______________________

MO TU WE TH FR SA SU
☐   ☐   ☐   ☐   ☐   ☐   ☐

DATE: /   /

PROJECT:

FOREMAN:

WEATHER

F°_____ C°_____   _____ AM   _____ PM

HOURS DUE TO BAD WEATHER

ISSUED AND DELAYS

NOTE: ____

COMPLETION DATE	DAYS AHEAD OF SCHEDULE	DAYS BEHIND SCHEDULE

SAFETY AND INCIDENTS

SAFETY ISSUES THAT NEED TO BE ADDRESSED	ACCIDENTS / INCIDENTS / STEPS NEEDED TO RESOLVE

SUMMARY OF THE WORK DONE TODAY

IMPORTANT NOTES

NAME	SIGNATURE

TODAY LABOR

INITIALS	TRADE	START	FINISH	PAID HOURS	OVERTIME	COMPANY
☐ EMPLOYEE ☐ CONTRUCTOR		AM	PM			
☐ EMPLOYEE ☐ CONTRUCTOR		AM	PM			
☐ EMPLOYEE ☐ CONTRUCTOR		AM	PM			
☐ EMPLOYEE ☐ CONTRUCTOR		AM	PM			
☐ EMPLOYEE ☐ CONTRUCTOR		AM	PM			
☐ EMPLOYEE ☐ CONTRUCTOR		AM	PM			
☐ EMPLOYEE ☐ CONTRUCTOR		AM	PM			
☐ EMPLOYEE ☐ CONTRUCTOR		AM	PM			

EQUIPMENT ON SITE	NO. OF UNITE	WORKING YES / NO

HIRED EQUIPMENT	NO. OF UNITE	EQUIPMENT RENTED	FROM	RATE

NAME: ___________________________   SIGNATURE: ___________________________

MO   TU   WE   TH   FR   SA   SU
☐   ☐   ☐   ☐   ☐   ☐   ☐

DATE: /   /

PROJECT:

FOREMAN:

WEATHER

F°_____   C°_____   _____ AM   _____ PM

HOURS DUE TO BAD WEATHER

ISSUED AND DELAYS

NOTE:

COMPLETION DATE	DAYS AHEAD OF SCHEDULE	DAYS BEHIND SCHEDULE

SAFETY AND INCIDENTS

SAFETY ISSUES THAT NEED TO BE ADDRESSED	ACCIDENTS / INCIDENTS / STEPS NEEDED TO RESOLVE

SUMMARY OF THE WORK DONE TODAY

IMPORTANT NOTES

NAME	SIGNATURE

TODAY LABOR

INITIALS	TRADE	START	FINISH	PAID HOURS	OVERTIME	COMPANY
☐ EMPLOYEE ☐ CONTRUCTOR		AM	PM			
☐ EMPLOYEE ☐ CONTRUCTOR		AM	PM			
☐ EMPLOYEE ☐ CONTRUCTOR		AM	PM			
☐ EMPLOYEE ☐ CONTRUCTOR		AM	PM			
☐ EMPLOYEE ☐ CONTRUCTOR		AM	PM			
☐ EMPLOYEE ☐ CONTRUCTOR		AM	PM			
☐ EMPLOYEE ☐ CONTRUCTOR		AM	PM			
☐ EMPLOYEE ☐ CONTRUCTOR		AM	PM			

EQUIPMENT ON SITE	NO. OF UNITE	WORKING YES / NO

HIRED EQUIPMENT	NO. OF UNITE	EQUIPMENT RENTED	FROM	RATE

NAME: _______________________________   SIGNATURE: _______________________________

MO   TU   WE   TH   FR   SA   SU
☐   ☐   ☐   ☐   ☐   ☐   ☐

DATE: ___ / ___ / ___

PROJECT:

FOREMAN:

WEATHER

F° _____ C° _____ _____ AM _____ PM

HOURS DUE TO BAD WEATHER

ISSUED AND DELAYS

NOTE: _______________________________

COMPLETION DATE	DAYS AHEAD OF SCHEDULE	DAYS BEHIND SCHEDULE

SAFETY AND INCIDENTS

SAFETY ISSUES THAT NEED TO BE ADDRESSED	ACCIDENTS / INCIDENTS / STEPS NEEDED TO RESOLVE

SUMMARY OF THE WORK DONE TODAY

IMPORTANT NOTES

NAME	SIGNATURE

<table>
<tr><td colspan="8" align="center">TODAY LABOR</td></tr>
<tr><td>INITIALS</td><td>TRADE</td><td>START</td><td>FINISH</td><td>PAID HOURS</td><td>OVERTIME</td><td>COMPANY</td></tr>
<tr><td>☐ EMPLOYEE
☐ CONTRUCTOR</td><td></td><td>AM</td><td>PM</td><td></td><td></td><td></td></tr>
<tr><td>☐ EMPLOYEE
☐ CONTRUCTOR</td><td></td><td>AM</td><td>PM</td><td></td><td></td><td></td></tr>
<tr><td>☐ EMPLOYEE
☐ CONTRUCTOR</td><td></td><td>AM</td><td>PM</td><td></td><td></td><td></td></tr>
<tr><td>☐ EMPLOYEE
☐ CONTRUCTOR</td><td></td><td>AM</td><td>PM</td><td></td><td></td><td></td></tr>
<tr><td>☐ EMPLOYEE
☐ CONTRUCTOR</td><td></td><td>AM</td><td>PM</td><td></td><td></td><td></td></tr>
<tr><td>☐ EMPLOYEE
☐ CONTRUCTOR</td><td></td><td>AM</td><td>PM</td><td></td><td></td><td></td></tr>
<tr><td>☐ EMPLOYEE
☐ CONTRUCTOR</td><td></td><td>AM</td><td>PM</td><td></td><td></td><td></td></tr>
<tr><td>☐ EMPLOYEE
☐ CONTRUCTOR</td><td></td><td>AM</td><td>PM</td><td></td><td></td><td></td></tr>
</table>

EQUIPMENT ON SITE	NO. OF UNITE	WORKING YES / NO

HIRED EQUIPMENT	NO. OF UNITE	EQUIPMENT RENTED	FROM	RATE

NAME: _______________________   SIGNATURE: _______________________

MO   TU   WE   TH   FR   SA   SU
☐   ☐   ☐   ☐   ☐   ☐   ☐

DATE: /   /

PROJECT:

FOREMAN:

WEATHER   F° _____   C° _____   _____ AM   _____ PM

HOURS DUE TO BAD WEATHER	ISSUED AND DELAYS

NOTE: _____________________________________

COMPLETION DATE	DAYS AHEAD OF SCHEDULE	DAYS BEHIND SCHEDULE

SAFETY AND INCIDENTS

SAFETY ISSUES THAT NEED TO BE ADDRESSED	ACCIDENTS / INCIDENTS / STEPS NEEDED TO RESOLVE

SUMMARY OF THE WORK DONE TODAY

IMPORTANT NOTES

NAME	SIGNATURE

<table>
<tr><td colspan="7" align="center">TODAY LABOR</td></tr>
<tr><td>INITIALS</td><td>TRADE</td><td>START</td><td>FINISH</td><td>PAID HOURS</td><td>OVERTIME</td><td>COMPANY</td></tr>
<tr><td>☐ EMPLOYEE
☐ CONTRUCTOR</td><td></td><td>AM</td><td>PM</td><td></td><td></td><td></td></tr>
<tr><td>☐ EMPLOYEE
☐ CONTRUCTOR</td><td></td><td>AM</td><td>PM</td><td></td><td></td><td></td></tr>
<tr><td>☐ EMPLOYEE
☐ CONTRUCTOR</td><td></td><td>AM</td><td>PM</td><td></td><td></td><td></td></tr>
<tr><td>☐ EMPLOYEE
☐ CONTRUCTOR</td><td></td><td>AM</td><td>PM</td><td></td><td></td><td></td></tr>
<tr><td>☐ EMPLOYEE
☐ CONTRUCTOR</td><td></td><td>AM</td><td>PM</td><td></td><td></td><td></td></tr>
<tr><td>☐ EMPLOYEE
☐ CONTRUCTOR</td><td></td><td>AM</td><td>PM</td><td></td><td></td><td></td></tr>
<tr><td>☐ EMPLOYEE
☐ CONTRUCTOR</td><td></td><td>AM</td><td>PM</td><td></td><td></td><td></td></tr>
<tr><td>☐ EMPLOYEE
☐ CONTRUCTOR</td><td></td><td>AM</td><td>PM</td><td></td><td></td><td></td></tr>
</table>

EQUIPMENT ON SITE	NO. OF UNITE	WORKING YES / NO

HIRED EQUIPMENT	NO. OF UNITE	EQUIPMENT RENTED	FROM	RATE

NAME: _______________________   SIGNATURE: _______________________

MO TU WE TH FR SA SU
☐   ☐   ☐   ☐   ☐   ☐   ☐

DATE: /   /

PROJECT:

FOREMAN:

WEATHER

F°_____ C°_____   _____ AM _____ PM

HOURS DUE TO
BAD WEATHER

ISSUED AND DELAYS

NOTE: ____

COMPLETION DATE	DAYS AHEAD OF SCHEDULE	DAYS BEHIND SCHEDULE

SAFETY AND INCIDENTS

SAFETY ISSUES THAT NEED TO BE ADDRESSED	ACCIDENTS / INCIDENTS / STEPS NEEDED TO RESOLVE

SUMMARY OF THE WORK DONE TODAY

IMPORTANT NOTES

NAME	SIGNATURE

TODAY LABOR

INITIALS	TRADE	START	FINISH	PAID HOURS	OVERTIME	COMPANY
☐ EMPLOYEE ☐ CONTRUCTOR		AM	PM			
☐ EMPLOYEE ☐ CONTRUCTOR		AM	PM			
☐ EMPLOYEE ☐ CONTRUCTOR		AM	PM			
☐ EMPLOYEE ☐ CONTRUCTOR		AM	PM			
☐ EMPLOYEE ☐ CONTRUCTOR		AM	PM			
☐ EMPLOYEE ☐ CONTRUCTOR		AM	PM			
☐ EMPLOYEE ☐ CONTRUCTOR		AM	PM			
☐ EMPLOYEE ☐ CONTRUCTOR		AM	PM			

EQUIPMENT ON SITE	NO. OF UNITE	WORKING YES / NO

HIRED EQUIPMENT	NO. OF UNITE	EQUIPMENT RENTED	FROM	RATE

NAME: _______________________________   SIGNATURE: _______________________________

MO TU WE TH FR SA SU

DATE: /   /

PROJECT:

FOREMAN:

WEATHER

F°_______ C°_______   _______ AM   _______ PM

HOURS DUE TO BAD WEATHER

ISSUED AND DELAYS

NOTE: _______

COMPLETION DATE	DAYS AHEAD OF SCHEDULE	DAYS BEHIND SCHEDULE

SAFETY AND INCIDENTS

SAFETY ISSUES THAT NEED TO BE ADDRESSED	ACCIDENTS / INCIDENTS / STEPS NEEDED TO RESOLVE

SUMMARY OF THE WORK DONE TODAY

IMPORTANT NOTES

NAME	SIGNATURE

TODAY LABOR

INITIALS	TRADE	START	FINISH	PAID HOURS	OVERTIME	COMPANY
☐ EMPLOYEE ☐ CONTRUCTOR		AM	PM			
☐ EMPLOYEE ☐ CONTRUCTOR		AM	PM			
☐ EMPLOYEE ☐ CONTRUCTOR		AM	PM			
☐ EMPLOYEE ☐ CONTRUCTOR		AM	PM			
☐ EMPLOYEE ☐ CONTRUCTOR		AM	PM			
☐ EMPLOYEE ☐ CONTRUCTOR		AM	PM			
☐ EMPLOYEE ☐ CONTRUCTOR		AM	PM			
☐ EMPLOYEE ☐ CONTRUCTOR		AM	PM			

EQUIPMENT ON SITE	NO. OF UNITE	WORKING YES / NO

HIRED EQUIPMENT	NO. OF UNITE	EQUIPMENT RENTED	FROM	RATE

NAME: _______________________________   SIGNATURE: _______________________________

MO TU WE TH FR SA SU
☐   ☐   ☐   ☐   ☐   ☐   ☐

DATE: __ / __ / __

PROJECT:

FOREMAN:

WEATHER

F°_____ C°_____ _____ AM _____ PM

HOURS DUE TO BAD WEATHER

ISSUED AND DELAYS

NOTE: _______________________________

COMPLETION DATE	DAYS AHEAD OF SCHEDULE	DAYS BEHIND SCHEDULE

SAFETY AND INCIDENTS

SAFETY ISSUES THAT NEED TO BE ADDRESSED	ACCIDENTS / INCIDENTS / STEPS NEEDED TO RESOLVE

SUMMARY OF THE WORK DONE TODAY

IMPORTANT NOTES

NAME	SIGNATURE

TODAY LABOR

INITIALS	TRADE	START	FINISH	PAID HOURS	OVERTIME	COMPANY
☐ EMPLOYEE ☐ CONTRUCTOR		AM	PM			
☐ EMPLOYEE ☐ CONTRUCTOR		AM	PM			
☐ EMPLOYEE ☐ CONTRUCTOR		AM	PM			
☐ EMPLOYEE ☐ CONTRUCTOR		AM	PM			
☐ EMPLOYEE ☐ CONTRUCTOR		AM	PM			
☐ EMPLOYEE ☐ CONTRUCTOR		AM	PM			
☐ EMPLOYEE ☐ CONTRUCTOR		AM	PM			
☐ EMPLOYEE ☐ CONTRUCTOR		AM	PM			

EQUIPMENT ON SITE	NO. OF UNITE	WORKING YES / NO

HIRED EQUIPMENT	NO. OF UNITE	EQUIPMENT RENTED	FROM	RATE

NAME: _______________________   SIGNATURE: _______________________

MO   TU   WE   TH   FR   SA   SU
☐   ☐   ☐   ☐   ☐   ☐   ☐

DATE: /   /

PROJECT:

FOREMAN:

WEATHER

F°____   C°____   ____ AM   ____ PM

HOURS DUE TO BAD WEATHER	ISSUED AND DELAYS

NOTE: ____

COMPLETION DATE	DAYS AHEAD OF SCHEDULE	DAYS BEHIND SCHEDULE

SAFETY AND INCIDENTS

SAFETY ISSUES THAT NEED TO BE ADDRESSED	ACCIDENTS / INCIDENTS / STEPS NEEDED TO RESOLVE

SUMMARY OF THE WORK DONE TODAY

IMPORTANT NOTES

NAME	SIGNATURE

<table>
<tr><td colspan="7" align="center">TODAY LABOR</td></tr>
<tr><td>INITIALS</td><td>TRADE</td><td>START</td><td>FINISH</td><td>PAID HOURS</td><td>OVERTIME</td><td>COMPANY</td></tr>
<tr><td>☐ EMPLOYEE
☐ CONTRUCTOR</td><td></td><td>AM</td><td>PM</td><td></td><td></td><td></td></tr>
<tr><td>☐ EMPLOYEE
☐ CONTRUCTOR</td><td></td><td>AM</td><td>PM</td><td></td><td></td><td></td></tr>
<tr><td>☐ EMPLOYEE
☐ CONTRUCTOR</td><td></td><td>AM</td><td>PM</td><td></td><td></td><td></td></tr>
<tr><td>☐ EMPLOYEE
☐ CONTRUCTOR</td><td></td><td>AM</td><td>PM</td><td></td><td></td><td></td></tr>
<tr><td>☐ EMPLOYEE
☐ CONTRUCTOR</td><td></td><td>AM</td><td>PM</td><td></td><td></td><td></td></tr>
<tr><td>☐ EMPLOYEE
☐ CONTRUCTOR</td><td></td><td>AM</td><td>PM</td><td></td><td></td><td></td></tr>
<tr><td>☐ EMPLOYEE
☐ CONTRUCTOR</td><td></td><td>AM</td><td>PM</td><td></td><td></td><td></td></tr>
<tr><td>☐ EMPLOYEE
☐ CONTRUCTOR</td><td></td><td>AM</td><td>PM</td><td></td><td></td><td></td></tr>
</table>

EQUIPMENT ON SITE	NO. OF UNITE	WORKING YES / NO

HIRED EQUIPMENT	NO. OF UNITE	EQUIPMENT RENTED	FROM	RATE

NAME: _______________________   SIGNATURE: _______________________

MO   TU   WE   TH   FR   SA   SU
☐   ☐   ☐   ☐   ☐   ☐   ☐

DATE: ___ / ___ / ___

PROJECT:

FOREMAN:

WEATHER

F° _____   C° _____   _____ AM   _____ PM

HOURS DUE TO BAD WEATHER

ISSUED AND DELAYS

NOTE: ____

COMPLETION DATE	DAYS AHEAD OF SCHEDULE	DAYS BEHIND SCHEDULE

SAFETY AND INCIDENTS

SAFETY ISSUES THAT NEED TO BE ADDRESSED	ACCIDENTS / INCIDENTS / STEPS NEEDED TO RESOLVE

SUMMARY OF THE WORK DONE TODAY

IMPORTANT NOTES

NAME	SIGNATURE

TODAY LABOR

INITIALS	TRADE	START	FINISH	PAID HOURS	OVERTIME	COMPANY
☐ EMPLOYEE ☐ CONTRUCTOR		AM	PM			
☐ EMPLOYEE ☐ CONTRUCTOR		AM	PM			
☐ EMPLOYEE ☐ CONTRUCTOR		AM	PM			
☐ EMPLOYEE ☐ CONTRUCTOR		AM	PM			
☐ EMPLOYEE ☐ CONTRUCTOR		AM	PM			
☐ EMPLOYEE ☐ CONTRUCTOR		AM	PM			
☐ EMPLOYEE ☐ CONTRUCTOR		AM	PM			
☐ EMPLOYEE ☐ CONTRUCTOR		AM	PM			

EQUIPMENT ON SITE	NO. OF UNITE	WORKING YES / NO

HIRED EQUIPMENT	NO. OF UNITE	EQUIPMENT RENTED	FROM	RATE

NAME: _______________________   SIGNATURE: _______________________

MO TU WE TH FR SA SU

DATE: ___ / ___ / ___

PROJECT:

FOREMAN:

WEATHER

F° ___ C° ___ ___ AM ___ PM

HOURS DUE TO BAD WEATHER

ISSUED AND DELAYS

NOTE: ___

COMPLETION DATE	DAYS AHEAD OF SCHEDULE	DAYS BEHIND SCHEDULE

SAFETY AND INCIDENTS

SAFETY ISSUES THAT NEED TO BE ADDRESSED	ACCIDENTS / INCIDENTS / STEPS NEEDED TO RESOLVE

SUMMARY OF THE WORK DONE TODAY

IMPORTANT NOTES

NAME	SIGNATURE

TODAY LABOR

INITIALS	TRADE	START	FINISH	PAID HOURS	OVERTIME	COMPANY
☐ EMPLOYEE ☐ CONTRUCTOR		AM	PM			
☐ EMPLOYEE ☐ CONTRUCTOR		AM	PM			
☐ EMPLOYEE ☐ CONTRUCTOR		AM	PM			
☐ EMPLOYEE ☐ CONTRUCTOR		AM	PM			
☐ EMPLOYEE ☐ CONTRUCTOR		AM	PM			
☐ EMPLOYEE ☐ CONTRUCTOR		AM	PM			
☐ EMPLOYEE ☐ CONTRUCTOR		AM	PM			
☐ EMPLOYEE ☐ CONTRUCTOR		AM	PM			

EQUIPMENT ON SITE	NO. OF UNITE	WORKING YES / NO

HIRED EQUIPMENT	NO. OF UNITE	EQUIPMENT RENTED	FROM	RATE

NAME: _______________________________   SIGNATURE: _______________________________

MO   TU   WE   TH   FR   SA   SU
☐   ☐   ☐   ☐   ☐   ☐   ☐

DATE: ___ / ___ / ___

PROJECT:

FOREMAN:

WEATHER   F° ____   C° ____   ____ AM   ____ PM

HOURS DUE TO BAD WEATHER	ISSUED AND DELAYS

NOTE: ____

COMPLETION DATE	DAYS AHEAD OF SCHEDULE	DAYS BEHIND SCHEDULE

SAFETY AND INCIDENTS

SAFETY ISSUES THAT NEED TO BE ADDRESSED	ACCIDENTS / INCIDENTS / STEPS NEEDED TO RESOLVE

SUMMARY OF THE WORK DONE TODAY

IMPORTANT NOTES

NAME	SIGNATURE

TODAY LABOR

INITIALS	TRADE	START	FINISH	PAID HOURS	OVERTIME	COMPANY
☐ EMPLOYEE ☐ CONTRUCTOR		AM	PM			
☐ EMPLOYEE ☐ CONTRUCTOR		AM	PM			
☐ EMPLOYEE ☐ CONTRUCTOR		AM	PM			
☐ EMPLOYEE ☐ CONTRUCTOR		AM	PM			
☐ EMPLOYEE ☐ CONTRUCTOR		AM	PM			
☐ EMPLOYEE ☐ CONTRUCTOR		AM	PM			
☐ EMPLOYEE ☐ CONTRUCTOR		AM	PM			
☐ EMPLOYEE ☐ CONTRUCTOR		AM	PM			

EQUIPMENT ON SITE	NO. OF UNITE	WORKING YES / NO

HIRED EQUIPMENT	NO. OF UNITE	EQUIPMENT RENTED	FROM	RATE

NAME: _______________________   SIGNATURE: _______________________

MO TU WE TH FR SA SU
☐   ☐   ☐   ☐   ☐   ☐   ☐

DATE: /   /

PROJECT:

FOREMAN:

WEATHER

F°_____ C°_____ _____AM _____PM

HOURS DUE TO BAD WEATHER

ISSUED AND DELAYS

NOTE:

COMPLETION DATE	DAYS AHEAD OF SCHEDULE	DAYS BEHIND SCHEDULE

SAFETY AND INCIDENTS

SAFETY ISSUES THAT NEED TO BE ADDRESSED	ACCIDENTS / INCIDENTS / STEPS NEEDED TO RESOLVE

SUMMARY OF THE WORK DONE TODAY

IMPORTANT NOTES

NAME	SIGNATURE

TODAY LABOR

INITIALS	TRADE	START	FINISH	PAID HOURS	OVERTIME	COMPANY
☐ EMPLOYEE ☐ CONTRUCTOR		AM	PM			
☐ EMPLOYEE ☐ CONTRUCTOR		AM	PM			
☐ EMPLOYEE ☐ CONTRUCTOR		AM	PM			
☐ EMPLOYEE ☐ CONTRUCTOR		AM	PM			
☐ EMPLOYEE ☐ CONTRUCTOR		AM	PM			
☐ EMPLOYEE ☐ CONTRUCTOR		AM	PM			
☐ EMPLOYEE ☐ CONTRUCTOR		AM	PM			
☐ EMPLOYEE ☐ CONTRUCTOR		AM	PM			

EQUIPMENT ON SITE	NO. OF UNITE	WORKING YES / NO

HIRED EQUIPMENT	NO. OF UNITE	EQUIPMENT RENTED	FROM	RATE

NAME: _______________________   SIGNATURE: _______________________

MO   TU   WE   TH   FR   SA   SU
☐   ☐   ☐   ☐   ☐   ☐   ☐

DATE: /   /

PROJECT:

FOREMAN:

WEATHER

F°______ C°______   ______ AM ______ PM

HOURS DUE TO BAD WEATHER

ISSUED AND DELAYS

NOTE: ____

COMPLETION DATE	DAYS AHEAD OF SCHEDULE	DAYS BEHIND SCHEDULE

SAFETY AND INCIDENTS

SAFETY ISSUES THAT NEED TO BE ADDRESSED	ACCIDENTS / INCIDENTS / STEPS NEEDED TO RESOLVE

SUMMARY OF THE WORK DONE TODAY

IMPORTANT NOTES

NAME	SIGNATURE

<table>
<tr><td colspan="8" align="center">TODAY LABOR</td></tr>
<tr><td>INITIALS</td><td>TRADE</td><td>START</td><td>FINISH</td><td>PAID HOURS</td><td>OVERTIME</td><td>COMPANY</td></tr>
<tr><td>☐ EMPLOYEE
☐ CONTRUCTOR</td><td></td><td>AM</td><td>PM</td><td></td><td></td><td></td></tr>
<tr><td>☐ EMPLOYEE
☐ CONTRUCTOR</td><td></td><td>AM</td><td>PM</td><td></td><td></td><td></td></tr>
<tr><td>☐ EMPLOYEE
☐ CONTRUCTOR</td><td></td><td>AM</td><td>PM</td><td></td><td></td><td></td></tr>
<tr><td>☐ EMPLOYEE
☐ CONTRUCTOR</td><td></td><td>AM</td><td>PM</td><td></td><td></td><td></td></tr>
<tr><td>☐ EMPLOYEE
☐ CONTRUCTOR</td><td></td><td>AM</td><td>PM</td><td></td><td></td><td></td></tr>
<tr><td>☐ EMPLOYEE
☐ CONTRUCTOR</td><td></td><td>AM</td><td>PM</td><td></td><td></td><td></td></tr>
<tr><td>☐ EMPLOYEE
☐ CONTRUCTOR</td><td></td><td>AM</td><td>PM</td><td></td><td></td><td></td></tr>
<tr><td>☐ EMPLOYEE
☐ CONTRUCTOR</td><td></td><td>AM</td><td>PM</td><td></td><td></td><td></td></tr>
</table>

EQUIPMENT ON SITE	NO. OF UNITE	WORKING YES / NO

HIRED EQUIPMENT	NO. OF UNITE	EQUIPMENT RENTED	FROM	RATE

NAME: ______________________   SIGNATURE: ______________________

MO	TU	WE	TH	FR	SA	SU
☐	☐	☐	☐	☐	☐	☐

DATE: ___ / ___ / ___

PROJECT: ___________________

FOREMAN: ___________________

WEATHER F°___ C°___ ___AM ___PM

| HOURS DUE TO BAD WEATHER | ISSUED AND DELAYS |

NOTE: ___________________

COMPLETION DATE	DAYS AHEAD OF SCHEDULE	DAYS BEHIND SCHEDULE

SAFETY AND INCIDENTS

SAFETY ISSUES THAT NEED TO BE ADDRESSED	ACCIDENTS / INCIDENTS / STEPS NEEDED TO RESOLVE

SUMMARY OF THE WORK DONE TODAY

IMPORTANT NOTES

NAME	SIGNATURE

TODAY LABOR

INITIALS	TRADE	START	FINISH	PAID HOURS	OVERTIME	COMPANY
☐ EMPLOYEE ☐ CONTRUCTOR		AM	PM			
☐ EMPLOYEE ☐ CONTRUCTOR		AM	PM			
☐ EMPLOYEE ☐ CONTRUCTOR		AM	PM			
☐ EMPLOYEE ☐ CONTRUCTOR		AM	PM			
☐ EMPLOYEE ☐ CONTRUCTOR		AM	PM			
☐ EMPLOYEE ☐ CONTRUCTOR		AM	PM			
☐ EMPLOYEE ☐ CONTRUCTOR		AM	PM			
☐ EMPLOYEE ☐ CONTRUCTOR		AM	PM			

EQUIPMENT ON SITE	NO. OF UNITE	WORKING YES / NO

HIRED EQUIPMENT	NO. OF UNITE	EQUIPMENT RENTED	FROM	RATE

NAME: _______________________ SIGNATURE: _______________________

MO TU WE TH FR SA SU
☐   ☐   ☐   ☐   ☐   ☐   ☐

DATE: __ / __ / __

PROJECT:

FOREMAN:

WEATHER

F° _____ C° _____   _____ AM _____ PM

HOURS DUE TO BAD WEATHER

ISSUED AND DELAYS

NOTE: ____

COMPLETION DATE	DAYS AHEAD OF SCHEDULE	DAYS BEHIND SCHEDULE

SAFETY AND INCIDENTS

SAFETY ISSUES THAT NEED TO BE ADDRESSED	ACCIDENTS / INCIDENTS / STEPS NEEDED TO RESOLVE

SUMMARY OF THE WORK DONE TODAY

IMPORTANT NOTES

NAME	SIGNATURE

TODAY LABOR

INITIALS	TRADE	START	FINISH	PAID HOURS	OVERTIME	COMPANY
☐ EMPLOYEE ☐ CONTRUCTOR		AM	PM			
☐ EMPLOYEE ☐ CONTRUCTOR		AM	PM			
☐ EMPLOYEE ☐ CONTRUCTOR		AM	PM			
☐ EMPLOYEE ☐ CONTRUCTOR		AM	PM			
☐ EMPLOYEE ☐ CONTRUCTOR		AM	PM			
☐ EMPLOYEE ☐ CONTRUCTOR		AM	PM			
☐ EMPLOYEE ☐ CONTRUCTOR		AM	PM			
☐ EMPLOYEE ☐ CONTRUCTOR		AM	PM			

EQUIPMENT ON SITE	NO. OF UNITE	WORKING YES / NO

HIRED EQUIPMENT	NO. OF UNITE	EQUIPMENT RENTED	FROM	RATE

NAME: _______________________   SIGNATURE: _______________________

MO   TU   WE   TH   FR   SA   SU
☐   ☐   ☐   ☐   ☐   ☐   ☐

DATE: /   /

PROJECT:

FOREMAN:

WEATHER

F°____ C°____   ____ AM ____ PM

HOURS DUE TO BAD WEATHER	ISSUED AND DELAYS

NOTE: ____

COMPLETION DATE	DAYS AHEAD OF SCHEDULE	DAYS BEHIND SCHEDULE

SAFETY AND INCIDENTS

SAFETY ISSUES THAT NEED TO BE ADDRESSED	ACCIDENTS / INCIDENTS / STEPS NEEDED TO RESOLVE

SUMMARY OF THE WORK DONE TODAY

____

____

____

____

IMPORTANT NOTES

____

____

____

____

NAME	SIGNATURE

<table>
<tr><th colspan="8" style="text-align:center">TODAY LABOR</th></tr>
<tr><th>INITIALS</th><th>TRADE</th><th>START</th><th>FINISH</th><th>PAID HOURS</th><th>OVERTIME</th><th>COMPANY</th></tr>
<tr><td>☐ EMPLOYEE
☐ CONTRUCTOR</td><td></td><td>AM</td><td>PM</td><td></td><td></td><td></td></tr>
<tr><td>☐ EMPLOYEE
☐ CONTRUCTOR</td><td></td><td>AM</td><td>PM</td><td></td><td></td><td></td></tr>
<tr><td>☐ EMPLOYEE
☐ CONTRUCTOR</td><td></td><td>AM</td><td>PM</td><td></td><td></td><td></td></tr>
<tr><td>☐ EMPLOYEE
☐ CONTRUCTOR</td><td></td><td>AM</td><td>PM</td><td></td><td></td><td></td></tr>
<tr><td>☐ EMPLOYEE
☐ CONTRUCTOR</td><td></td><td>AM</td><td>PM</td><td></td><td></td><td></td></tr>
<tr><td>☐ EMPLOYEE
☐ CONTRUCTOR</td><td></td><td>AM</td><td>PM</td><td></td><td></td><td></td></tr>
<tr><td>☐ EMPLOYEE
☐ CONTRUCTOR</td><td></td><td>AM</td><td>PM</td><td></td><td></td><td></td></tr>
<tr><td>☐ EMPLOYEE
☐ CONTRUCTOR</td><td></td><td>AM</td><td>PM</td><td></td><td></td><td></td></tr>
</table>

EQUIPMENT ON SITE	NO. OF UNITE	WORKING YES / NO

HIRED EQUIPMENT	NO. OF UNITE	EQUIPMENT RENTED	FROM	RATE

NAME: ________________________   SIGNATURE: ________________________

MO   TU   WE   TH   FR   SA   SU
☐   ☐   ☐   ☐   ☐   ☐   ☐

DATE: /   /

PROJECT:

FOREMAN:

WEATHER

F°_____ C°_____   _____ AM   _____ PM

HOURS DUE TO
BAD WEATHER

ISSUED AND DELAYS

NOTE: _______________________________________

COMPLETION DATE	DAYS AHEAD OF SCHEDULE	DAYS BEHIND SCHEDULE

SAFETY AND INCIDENTS

SAFETY ISSUES THAT NEED TO BE ADDRESSED	ACCIDENTS / INCIDENTS / STEPS NEEDED TO RESOLVE

SUMMARY OF THE WORK DONE TODAY

IMPORTANT NOTES

NAME	SIGNATURE

TODAY LABOR

INITIALS	TRADE	START	FINISH	PAID HOURS	OVERTIME	COMPANY
☐ EMPLOYEE ☐ CONTRUCTOR		AM	PM			
☐ EMPLOYEE ☐ CONTRUCTOR		AM	PM			
☐ EMPLOYEE ☐ CONTRUCTOR		AM	PM			
☐ EMPLOYEE ☐ CONTRUCTOR		AM	PM			
☐ EMPLOYEE ☐ CONTRUCTOR		AM	PM			
☐ EMPLOYEE ☐ CONTRUCTOR		AM	PM			
☐ EMPLOYEE ☐ CONTRUCTOR		AM	PM			
☐ EMPLOYEE ☐ CONTRUCTOR		AM	PM			

EQUIPMENT ON SITE	NO. OF UNITE	WORKING YES / NO

HIRED EQUIPMENT	NO. OF UNITE	EQUIPMENT RENTED	FROM	RATE

NAME: _______________________   SIGNATURE: _______________________

MO   TU   WE   TH   FR   SA   SU
☐   ☐   ☐   ☐   ☐   ☐   ☐

DATE: /   /

PROJECT:

FOREMAN:

WEATHER

F°_______   C°_______   _______ AM   _______ PM

HOURS DUE TO
BAD WEATHER

ISSUED AND DELAYS

NOTE:

COMPLETION DATE	DAYS AHEAD OF SCHEDULE	DAYS BEHIND SCHEDULE

SAFETY AND INCIDENTS

SAFETY ISSUES THAT NEED TO BE ADDRESSED	ACCIDENTS / INCIDENTS / STEPS NEEDED TO RESOLVE

SUMMARY OF THE WORK DONE TODAY

IMPORTANT NOTES

NAME	SIGNATURE

TODAY LABOR

INITIALS	TRADE	START	FINISH	PAID HOURS	OVERTIME	COMPANY
☐ EMPLOYEE ☐ CONTRUCTOR		AM	PM			
☐ EMPLOYEE ☐ CONTRUCTOR		AM	PM			
☐ EMPLOYEE ☐ CONTRUCTOR		AM	PM			
☐ EMPLOYEE ☐ CONTRUCTOR		AM	PM			
☐ EMPLOYEE ☐ CONTRUCTOR		AM	PM			
☐ EMPLOYEE ☐ CONTRUCTOR		AM	PM			
☐ EMPLOYEE ☐ CONTRUCTOR		AM	PM			
☐ EMPLOYEE ☐ CONTRUCTOR		AM	PM			

EQUIPMENT ON SITE	NO. OF UNITE	WORKING YES / NO

HIRED EQUIPMENT	NO. OF UNITE	EQUIPMENT RENTED	FROM	RATE

NAME: _______________________   SIGNATURE: _______________________

MO   TU   WE   TH   FR   SA   SU
☐   ☐   ☐   ☐   ☐   ☐   ☐

DATE: ___ / ___ / ___

PROJECT:

FOREMAN:

WEATHER   F° ____   C° ____   ____ AM   ____ PM

HOURS DUE TO BAD WEATHER	ISSUED AND DELAYS

NOTE: ____________________

COMPLETION DATE	DAYS AHEAD OF SCHEDULE	DAYS BEHIND SCHEDULE

SAFETY AND INCIDENTS

SAFETY ISSUES THAT NEED TO BE ADDRESSED	ACCIDENTS / INCIDENTS / STEPS NEEDED TO RESOLVE

SUMMARY OF THE WORK DONE TODAY

IMPORTANT NOTES

NAME	SIGNATURE

TODAY LABOR

INITIALS	TRADE	START	FINISH	PAID HOURS	OVERTIME	COMPANY
☐ EMPLOYEE ☐ CONTRUCTOR		AM	PM			
☐ EMPLOYEE ☐ CONTRUCTOR		AM	PM			
☐ EMPLOYEE ☐ CONTRUCTOR		AM	PM			
☐ EMPLOYEE ☐ CONTRUCTOR		AM	PM			
☐ EMPLOYEE ☐ CONTRUCTOR		AM	PM			
☐ EMPLOYEE ☐ CONTRUCTOR		AM	PM			
☐ EMPLOYEE ☐ CONTRUCTOR		AM	PM			
☐ EMPLOYEE ☐ CONTRUCTOR		AM	PM			

EQUIPMENT ON SITE	NO. OF UNITE	WORKING YES / NO

HIRED EQUIPMENT	NO. OF UNITE	EQUIPMENT RENTED	FROM	RATE

NAME: _______________________ SIGNATURE: _______________________

MO   TU   WE   TH   FR   SA   SU
☐   ☐   ☐   ☐   ☐   ☐   ☐

DATE: ___ / ___ / ___

PROJECT:

FOREMAN:

WEATHER

F°_____ C°_____   _____ AM _____ PM

HOURS DUE TO BAD WEATHER

ISSUED AND DELAYS

NOTE: ____

COMPLETION DATE	DAYS AHEAD OF SCHEDULE	DAYS BEHIND SCHEDULE

SAFETY AND INCIDENTS

SAFETY ISSUES THAT NEED TO BE ADDRESSED	ACCIDENTS / INCIDENTS / STEPS NEEDED TO RESOLVE

SUMMARY OF THE WORK DONE TODAY

IMPORTANT NOTES

NAME	SIGNATURE

<table>
<tr><th colspan="7" align="center">TODAY LABOR</th></tr>
<tr><th>INITIALS</th><th>TRADE</th><th>START</th><th>FINISH</th><th>PAID HOURS</th><th>OVERTIME</th><th>COMPANY</th></tr>
<tr><td>☐ EMPLOYEE
☐ CONTRUCTOR</td><td></td><td>AM</td><td>PM</td><td></td><td></td><td></td></tr>
<tr><td>☐ EMPLOYEE
☐ CONTRUCTOR</td><td></td><td>AM</td><td>PM</td><td></td><td></td><td></td></tr>
<tr><td>☐ EMPLOYEE
☐ CONTRUCTOR</td><td></td><td>AM</td><td>PM</td><td></td><td></td><td></td></tr>
<tr><td>☐ EMPLOYEE
☐ CONTRUCTOR</td><td></td><td>AM</td><td>PM</td><td></td><td></td><td></td></tr>
<tr><td>☐ EMPLOYEE
☐ CONTRUCTOR</td><td></td><td>AM</td><td>PM</td><td></td><td></td><td></td></tr>
<tr><td>☐ EMPLOYEE
☐ CONTRUCTOR</td><td></td><td>AM</td><td>PM</td><td></td><td></td><td></td></tr>
<tr><td>☐ EMPLOYEE
☐ CONTRUCTOR</td><td></td><td>AM</td><td>PM</td><td></td><td></td><td></td></tr>
<tr><td>☐ EMPLOYEE
☐ CONTRUCTOR</td><td></td><td>AM</td><td>PM</td><td></td><td></td><td></td></tr>
</table>

EQUIPMENT ON SITE	NO. OF UNITE	WORKING YES / NO

HIRED EQUIPMENT	NO. OF UNITE	EQUIPMENT RENTED	FROM	RATE

NAME: ______________________________   SIGNATURE: ______________________________

MO   TU   WE   TH   FR   SA   SU
☐   ☐   ☐   ☐   ☐   ☐   ☐

DATE: /   /

PROJECT:

FOREMAN:

WEATHER

F°_____ C°_____   _____ AM   _____ PM

HOURS DUE TO BAD WEATHER

ISSUED AND DELAYS

NOTE: ____

COMPLETION DATE	DAYS AHEAD OF SCHEDULE	DAYS BEHIND SCHEDULE

SAFETY AND INCIDENTS

SAFETY ISSUES THAT NEED TO BE ADDRESSED	ACCIDENTS / INCIDENTS / STEPS NEEDED TO RESOLVE

SUMMARY OF THE WORK DONE TODAY

IMPORTANT NOTES

NAME	SIGNATURE

<table>
<tr><td colspan="8" align="center">TODAY LABOR</td></tr>
<tr><td>INITIALS</td><td>TRADE</td><td>START</td><td>FINISH</td><td>PAID HOURS</td><td>OVERTIME</td><td>COMPANY</td></tr>
<tr><td>☐ EMPLOYEE
☐ CONTRUCTOR</td><td></td><td>AM</td><td>PM</td><td></td><td></td><td></td></tr>
<tr><td>☐ EMPLOYEE
☐ CONTRUCTOR</td><td></td><td>AM</td><td>PM</td><td></td><td></td><td></td></tr>
<tr><td>☐ EMPLOYEE
☐ CONTRUCTOR</td><td></td><td>AM</td><td>PM</td><td></td><td></td><td></td></tr>
<tr><td>☐ EMPLOYEE
☐ CONTRUCTOR</td><td></td><td>AM</td><td>PM</td><td></td><td></td><td></td></tr>
<tr><td>☐ EMPLOYEE
☐ CONTRUCTOR</td><td></td><td>AM</td><td>PM</td><td></td><td></td><td></td></tr>
<tr><td>☐ EMPLOYEE
☐ CONTRUCTOR</td><td></td><td>AM</td><td>PM</td><td></td><td></td><td></td></tr>
<tr><td>☐ EMPLOYEE
☐ CONTRUCTOR</td><td></td><td>AM</td><td>PM</td><td></td><td></td><td></td></tr>
<tr><td>☐ EMPLOYEE
☐ CONTRUCTOR</td><td></td><td>AM</td><td>PM</td><td></td><td></td><td></td></tr>
</table>

EQUIPMENT ON SITE	NO. OF UNITE	WORKING YES / NO

HIRED EQUIPMENT	NO. OF UNITE	EQUIPMENT RENTED	FROM	RATE

NAME: _______________________   SIGNATURE: _______________________

<table>
<tr><td>MO</td><td>TU</td><td>WE</td><td>TH</td><td>FR</td><td>SA</td><td>SU</td></tr>
<tr><td>☐</td><td>☐</td><td>☐</td><td>☐</td><td>☐</td><td>☐</td><td>☐</td></tr>
</table>

DATE: ___ / ___ / ___

PROJECT:

FOREMAN:

WEATHER   F°_____   C°_____   _____ AM   _____ PM

HOURS DUE TO BAD WEATHER	ISSUED AND DELAYS

NOTE: ____

COMPLETION DATE	DAYS AHEAD OF SCHEDULE	DAYS BEHIND SCHEDULE

SAFETY AND INCIDENTS

SAFETY ISSUES THAT NEED TO BE ADDRESSED	ACCIDENTS / INCIDENTS / STEPS NEEDED TO RESOLVE

SUMMARY OF THE WORK DONE TODAY

IMPORTANT NOTES

NAME	SIGNATURE

TODAY LABOR

INITIALS	TRADE	START	FINISH	PAID HOURS	OVERTIME	COMPANY
☐ EMPLOYEE ☐ CONTRUCTOR		AM	PM			
☐ EMPLOYEE ☐ CONTRUCTOR		AM	PM			
☐ EMPLOYEE ☐ CONTRUCTOR		AM	PM			
☐ EMPLOYEE ☐ CONTRUCTOR		AM	PM			
☐ EMPLOYEE ☐ CONTRUCTOR		AM	PM			
☐ EMPLOYEE ☐ CONTRUCTOR		AM	PM			
☐ EMPLOYEE ☐ CONTRUCTOR		AM	PM			
☐ EMPLOYEE ☐ CONTRUCTOR		AM	PM			

EQUIPMENT ON SITE	NO. OF UNITE	WORKING YES / NO

HIRED EQUIPMENT	NO. OF UNITE	EQUIPMENT RENTED	FROM	RATE

NAME: ________________________   SIGNATURE: ________________________

MO TU WE TH FR SA SU
☐   ☐   ☐   ☐   ☐   ☐   ☐

DATE: /   /

PROJECT:

FOREMAN:

WEATHER

F°_____ C°_____ _____ AM _____ PM

HOURS DUE TO BAD WEATHER

ISSUED AND DELAYS

NOTE: _______________________________________

COMPLETION DATE	DAYS AHEAD OF SCHEDULE	DAYS BEHIND SCHEDULE

SAFETY AND INCIDENTS

SAFETY ISSUES THAT NEED TO BE ADDRESSED	ACCIDENTS / INCIDENTS / STEPS NEEDED TO RESOLVE

SUMMARY OF THE WORK DONE TODAY

IMPORTANT NOTES

NAME	SIGNATURE